SYMPOSIUM

Nikos Kazantzakis

SYMPOSIUM

Translated by
Theodora Vasils and Themi Vasils

Thomas Y. Crowell Company
New York
Established 1834

Acknowledgment is made to Simon & Schuster, Inc. for permission to quote from *Nikos Kazantzakis—A Biography* by Helen Kazantzakis, page 91.

Designed by Ingrid Beckman

Manufactured in the United States of America

Library of Congress Cataloging in Publication Data

Kazantzakis, Nikos, 1883–1957.
    Symposium.

    I. Title.
PA5610.K39S913 1975   889′.3′32   74–18393
ISBN 0-690-00581-4
ISBN 0-308-10133-2 (Minerva paperback)

1 2 3 4 5 6 7 8 9 10

TRANSLATORS' NOTE

We are indebted to Mrs. Helen Kazantzakis for her assistance in providing us with references and answers to our many questions, and for her gracious help in general regarding this work. We are grateful also to the Reverend Evagoras Constantinides for the painstaking task of checking the finished translation with us, and for his helpful suggestions and assistance with certain passages. We are also grateful to Dr. Julia W. Loomis for her careful reading of the finished work and her helpful suggestions; to Julia Vasils for her invaluable knowledge of various idiomatic words and phrases; to Dr. George Anastaplo for his helpful comments; and to Litsa Dalageorgas for her assistance in facilitating some of our research on Kazantzakis' contemporaries.

In preparing the English translation we have used the first Greek edition of *Symposium*, published in Athens in 1971, edited by Mr. Emmanuel H. Kasdaglis, who worked from the original Kazantzakis manuscript at the Historical Museum of Heraklion in Crete, and from the typewritten copy of this manuscript sent to him by Helen Kazantzakis. We have attempted to remain as faithful as possible to the original Greek text and have followed its general format, including paragraphing, the capitalization of certain words, and the Greek usage of dashes to indicate dialogue instead of quotation marks.

THEODORA VASILS *and* THEMI VASILS

CONTENTS

SYMPOSIUM

INTRODUCTION

THE *Symposium*, although one of the earliest of Kazantzakis' works, curiously never appeared in published form until fourteen years after the writer's death. This "forgotten" work, which illuminates the source of many later Kazantzakis masterpieces, was acclaimed enthusiastically upon its appearance in Greece in 1971.

We are informed by Emmanuel H. Kasdaglis,[1] who edited the Greek published text, that the handwritten manuscript was found in the safe of Kazantzakis' father, Mihali Kazantzakis, after his death in 1932. Relatives gave the manuscript to Kazantzakis' nephew, Nikos Saklampanis,[2] then a young law student, as a memento of his uncle who was traveling in Spain at the time. Mr. Saklampanis kept it safe through the difficult war years and only recently turned it over to the Historical Museum of Heraklion, where it is now kept in the Kazantzakis Room with other manuscripts and mementos of the writer.

Before giving it to the museum, Mr. Saklampanis had a typewritten copy made of the manuscript and sent it to his aunt, Helen Kazantzakis in Geneva, Switzerland. It was this typewritten copy that Mr. Kasdaglis used, together with the original manuscript at the Heraklion Museum, to publish the *Symposium* in Athens in the summer of 1971. In editing the work, Mr. Kasdaglis took into consideration the handwritten corrections by Kazantzakis in two successive revisions of the handwritten manuscript made at a later date. Mr. Kasdaglis tells us that the manuscript has crossed-out portions throughout, as though the writer had used these portions elsewhere. And, indeed, there are, as he points out, echoes of the *Symposium* in other books of his, even identical phrases.[3]

Curiously, very little mention is made of the *Symposium*, either by the writer himself or by his friends and associates. Mr. Kasdaglis cites the almost simultaneous absorption of Kazantzakis at that time in the *Saviors of God*, which he completed a few months later, and in *Buddha*, and the *Odyssey*, which he began to write at the end of 1924, as reasons why Kazantzakis may have forgotten the *Symposium*.[4]

We know by a letter from Kazantzakis to his friend, the Rev. Emmanuel Papastefanou, who was living in Toledo, Ohio at that time that Kazantzakis had started writing the *Symposium* by 1922.

We also have references to this work in Helen Kazantzakis' biography of her husband.[5]

Pandelis Prevelakis,[6] who supervised the publication of Kazantzakis' complete works, provides us with another reference to the *Symposium*. In his essay, *The Poet and the Poem of the Odyssey* (Athens, 1958, pp. 290–291), and also in his essay, *Kazantzakis—Esoteric Biographical Sketch*, which prefaces his book *Four Hundred Letters of Kazantzakis to Prevelakis* (Athens, 1965), Prevelakis briefly summarizes the *Symposium* and identifies the persons at the dinner. He estimates that it was written around 1924–1925.

Helen Kazantzakis believes her husband had begun to write the *Symposium* in Vienna in 1922. She cites the date, September 5, 1922, on Kazantzakis' letter[7] to the Rev. Papastefanou, which was five days after he arrived in Berlin, as her reason for believing he had already started writing it in Vienna. In sending us copies of an exchange of letters between the two men, including the above letter of September 5, 1922, she notes: "I am sending you the entire letter, as well as two letters by Emmanuel Papastefanou so that you may understand in what a religious fervor they were living, and how different were their natures and their visions of God!"[8]

Entries in Kazantzakis' notebook at that time testify to this religious fervor. They reflect his abhorrence of the decadence in Vienna, the shame of modern life, and presage the savage warning of Arpagos in the *Symposium*: "It's time for the uproarious feast to break up, oh, Babylon, and for the lash to whistle in the air, and for that enormous spark, my spirit, to pounce on your buttresses and rush through your streets, burning your wooden gods and melting the golden calves and twisting your entrails . . ."

It appears from the letter to the Rev. Papastefanou that Kazantzakis had planned to include him in his *Symposium*, but in the revised version he has omitted him. It is Mrs. Kazantzakis' belief that the Papastefanou letters were too "romantic,"[9] and Kazantzakis abandoned the idea of including him as one of the *Symposium* participants. In the final draft, the participants, according to Pandelis Prevelakis are: Nikos Kazantzakis (Arpagos),[10] Angelos Sikelianos (Petros), Ion Dragoumis (Kosmas), and Myros Gunalakis (Myros). All but one were well-known figures in the Greek political and literary world.

Briefly summarized, the *Symposium* centers around the "confession" of Arpagos at a reunion dinner, hosted by him at his seaside house, and attended by his boyhood friends, Kosmas, Petros, and Myros. At their urgings, he launches into a confession that describes his agonizing search for liberation. In choppy, poetic strokes, at times the visionary, at others the zealous convert awkwardly unburdening his soul, he figuratively spans eternity in a confession that embodies the core of Kazantzakis' philosophy, and that is to ultimately reemerge as the nucleus of *Report to Greco*.

Of his three guests at the dinner, the major protagonists would appear to be Kosmas, symbolizing Ion Dragoumis,[11] the man of action, and Petros, symbolizing Angelos Sikelianos,[12] the poet. Myros, representing Myros Gunalakis, an old friend and colleague of Kazantzakis, plays the role of loyal and perceptive friend, and is the only dinner guest of the three whom Arpagos, out of compassion, refrains from rebuking. A childhood friend and schoolmate of Kazantzakis in Crete, he remained a friend throughout their early adult life and is known to have accompanied Kazantzakis to Switzerland in 1917. Referred to by Mr. Kasdaglis as "the unsuccessful Hunter of the absolute," he later became a successful businessman until his death in 1969.

A more formidable protagonist was Ion Dragoumis, one of the major Greek political figures of his day. Diplomat, politician, and writer, he exercised a profound influence, not only on the Greek political life of his time but also on his literary and intellectual peers. He wrote several books under the pseudonym Idas,[13] among them the well-known *Blood of Martyrs and Heroes*, written in 1907. It is a politically oriented work, inspired by the Macedonian struggle, in the style of the great Greek poet Palamas. In 1909 he produced *Samothrace*, and in 1911, *All Those Living*,* both works with political overtones. (That same year, Kazantzakis, while yet a student, wrote *The Masterbuilder*, a one-act tragedy, which he dedicated to Dragoumis). Deeply committed to the cause of combining theory with political action, Dragoumis was the central figure of a group of patriotic intellectuals with similar ideals.

It is this "man of action" that Arpagos lauds[14] so lavishly later in the *Symposium*, yet rebukes, because he has not learned to live the "integral purpose" that his struggles served. "You want to exorcise the ennui of life with danger," he warns, "and you don't understand it is not in your power to escape . . . that you serve an end superior to you." For Arpagos, action

*See Introduction, Note 7—reference by Kazantzakis to *All Those Living*.

ultimately becomes meaningless unless it is in conscious harmony with the superior purpose it serves.

The other protagonist, one of the major poets to emerge out of the dilemma that was facing Greek literature and art at the turn of the century, was Angelos Sikelianos. Pulled by the force of Western philosophy and literature, yet bound by the even stronger ties of a living national tradition, Greek writers and poets were searching for ways to synthesize the influence of the West with their own Greek tradition. This search was to find fertile ground in the work of Angelos Sikelianos, the man Kazantzakis chose to symbolize the poet in his *Symposium.*

In describing their first meeting in 1914, Kazantzakis refers to the "lightning-bolt" effect the eagle-eyed Sikelianos had on him. Laughter, nobility, a marvel of spiritual beauty, freshness. Their recognition of kinship was instantaneous. There followed a pilgrimage to Mount Athos—a highly charged, ecstatic, and anguished forty days of roaming through the sacred mountain, "living their Race and the faith of their fathers." Kazantzakis' notebook is filled with firsthand impressions and insights that were to appear later in the dialogues of the *Symposium* . . . references to asceticism, Buddha, Christ, Eros, Nature, Plato, and the gendarme who heard the words of Christ and became a monk because Christ's words "seemed sweeter than honey."

After Mount Athos there followed a historical pilgrimage through the Peloponnesos, to discover the "consciousness of their history." Kazantzakis was to say later that he owed much of the evolution in his thoughts to the company of Sikelianos on this trip.

In time the concepts shared in those early years were to change, grow firmer, take on new dimensions. While Sikelianos turned to Delphi for inspiration, Kazantzakis looked to Lenin as the future Savior of the world. For him the new Pythia had taken residence in Russia, but he was to grow disillusioned, and soon abandoned the hope of finding the god he was seeking in that direction.

By late 1922 he had begun to see a god who wanted to transcend Hope, "the last form of combat." An entry in his notebook,* dated December 4, 1922, records portions of a letter to his friend, Sikelianos: "I too am thinking of you. I too live in fervent expectation, awaiting the fruits of your victory. However, our paths have diverged. Not because at a difficult moment you distrusted the purity of my judgement; nor because you have forgotten all our resolutions and resumed the old path. These pusillanimities belong to the human part of our existence and are insignificant, ephemeral, without any weight for anyone

*Nikos Kazantzakis—A Biography, by Helen Kazantzakis, page 91 (New York: Simon & Schuster, 1968).

who sees beyond detail and temporality . . . . But because I sense that God is sinking more and more into the desert and wants to transcend the last form of combat, Hope."

No doubt both men were profoundly influenced by one another. They both shared a concept of the "supreme responsibility," although they did not agree on the methods of fulfilling it. Fundamental differences are echoed in their counterparts, Arpagos and Petros, in the *Symposium*: ". . . you shriek like an ailing man," warns Arpagos, in rebuking Petros for not creating the kind of poetry that could change men's lives. ". . . You shout of weariness, grief, ennui, and now, swayed by the winds of Frankish Europe, you warm over the dead gods. But the Franks are gone . . . and the supreme Responsibility is again in Anatolia, on our soil, to give new meaning and life and hope!"

For Sikelianos, the supreme responsibility is a challenge and a duty to preserve and perpetuate the living tradition of his Race. Nourished by the ever-thinning thread of a tradition that stretched fragilely back into the ancient world, he saw a need to trace this legend and folklore, the ancient songs and dances to their origin, to illuminate their source and awaken an awareness in others. As Edmund Keeley and Philip Sherrard tell us, in their introduction to *Six Poets of Modern Greece*,[15] Sikelianos was fortunate to have been born in Greece when the traditional memory and way of life was still very much alive. In searching for the source of this tradition, Messrs. Keeley and Sherrard tell us, Sikelianos turned to pre-Socratic Greece, to Orphism, the teachings of Pythagoras, the mysteries of Eleusis, Pindar, and Aeschylus, where he felt the art, beliefs, and customs of the Greek people had been consciously defined.

It would be absurd to believe that any modern Greek writer could or would escape the influence of so profound and awesome a legacy as the Greek tradition. Like Sikelianos, Kazantzakis drew deeply from Greek mythology. Dionysian-Appolonian imagery pervades much of his work, and though more inclined toward the world of Eleusis than that of the agora, he could hardly be exempt from the influence of Greek philosophy as well. His early translations of Platonic works tend to testify to his interest in the ancients. To what extent his work might have been influenced by them is a matter of speculation. His *Symposium*, like that other modern sequel, the *Odyssey*, draws from its classic prototype, but without any of the slavish imitation he so despised. The temptation to compare the Kazantzakis work with the Platonic prototype can hardly be ignored. Certainly there are similarities in structure, and perallels and contrasts worth noting.

Perhaps one of the more immediate contrasts is

that of intellectual climate, and the resulting tone of each work—Plato's reflecting the confidence and harmony of classical Greek thought, and Kazantzakis' reflecting his distrust of ready-made harmonies, which he rejects as ephemeral illusions. In Plato's world, aristocratic men of leisure can still indulge seriously in the ennobling pursuit of philosophical discourse. His characters, in a festive mood over Agathon's prize-winning play, reverberate with high good spirits and light banter. There is joy and humor in their discourse, an easy self-assurance and faith in man's place in the universe. In contrast, Kazantzakis' work exudes an almost harsh intensity, a profound and anguished seriousness, paradoxically blended with a Hessean mysticism. His world is all in flux, there is a search for new meanings. Greece, still reeling from the ravages of war and the not too distant four hundred years of enslavement under Turkish domination, is floundering. Arpagos voices the agony of his peers: "I seek to find the heart, the beginning and end, the purpose of Hellas, where every voice will find and take its place, that not a drop of strength and grace be lost. I seek the essence of the struggle—God."

Pandelis Prevelakis has called the Kazantzakis *Symposium* a summary, if not the nucleus, of *Report to Greco*. Written almost simultaneously with *The*

Saviors of God, a parallel spiritual work embodying the core of his philosophy in a formalized, hierarchical structure, it also appears to be the spontaneous raw material from which the latter emerged, a nubile creed.

Theodora Vasils
January 1974
Oak Park, Illinois

I
SYMPOSIUM

A GENTLE NIGHT BREEZE blew in from the sea cooling the parched earth. For a fleeting moment a seagull took flight, balanced its wings and hovered in the air; then in a sudden swoop toward the sea, it pierced the water's surface with its right wing, flapped about a few times and settled, with feet together, on the waves.

In the distance two dolphins vaulted suddenly, their sleek plump bodies glistening in the dusk, then abruptly vanished in a dive and reappeared beyond, floating side by side with upturned tails.

Oleanders had blossomed around Arpagos' little seaside house, filling the air with the pungent scent of bitter almonds. The friends who had come a long way were seated outside on the terrace, around the cleared table, and were silent.

"Kyrie . . . Kyrie . . ."[1] murmured Arpagos softly to himself, ashamed of being overheard.

The sun was now sinking into the waters and disappearing, and an azure darkness softly rose from the gullies and plains; for a moment the mountain slopes gleamed, then all the light gathered on the peak of the opposite mountain and, in a sudden leap toward the sky, disappeared. Everything in the azure air—stones and trees and people—breathed in god-given serenity, like symbols.

And the four hearts outside the modest house shuddered.

And Arpagos, quivering with mystical awe, whispered to himself, secretly, as though he alone were being initiated into the night's mystery:

"I've eaten from the drum, I've drunk from the cymbal, I've tasted from the cornucopia, I've burrowed in the bridal chamber. Demeter, oh, source of souls, the kernel of wheat that you entrusted to me died inside me, obeying your divine command and, look, the holy ear of wheat sprouts in multiblossoming fruit. And I feel your Daughter's fingers, like five springs, moving about on the top of my head, parting my hair and pouring strength, hope, patience, silence, and death."

—Arpagos, your lips are moving, said Kosmas, smiling. You're praying. Don't be embarrassed, we all know your secret now. The moment I faced you this morning and saw your serene face glowing and your glance falling upon us condescendingly, warm and tranquil and so distant, I said: Arpagos is lost. The deadly sea of divinity has swept him up, his brilliant mind has clouded, and we've set out in vain to take him with us to the city to fight. You broke the oath we took when we were still youths, Arpagos, and you threw away the shield!

Arpagos' sister, Helen, the modest young girl who was serving them, got up uneasily. She sensed the storm would break now. Since morning, the four friends, who were meeting today after so many years, had been feeling anxious and uneasy—the impersonal and still immature drives that united them as youths had been pruned by time and each had retained different ones, that hardened as they matured. She cut a blossoming branch of oleander, placed it on the center of the table, and sat down again. All day she had been trying to make them laugh, to soften their words and place a smile on the impatient will. But she couldn't go on. Toward evening the tension mounted and as the meal was coming to an end her heart began to tremble. A power, inexpressibly gentle, was draining from her, fighting to soothe the men and lighten the tension.

She looked at her brother entreatingly, but before

she could lean over and whisper, "Arpagos, Arpagos, don't knit your brows . . . be nice!" Petros had already begun to speak:

—Arpagos, you've welcomed us like a Homeric king, reviving the divine verses. We've bathed in the sea, played *lithari*,[2] basked in the sand, laughed, sung the old tunes, filled our glasses with eternal wine. And your simple table sparkled like a Symposium. But now, obeying the higher law of hospitality, with rigid antennas, like insects that have merged and want to be friends or die, we search your soul. What have you accomplished since we separated? How have you kept your word? Remember, we were joined together around a table then, too, and with that irrational, divine impudence of youth we swore that each of us, from somewhere, would demolish the world and then rebuild it. Now we laugh, because we've grown decadent. But then we trembled with God-inspired passion. And you withdrew into silence and disappeared in barren ascetic discipline. But the new Thebes blazes only in the cities now, and only there is it worthy for man to defeat the Tempter. Flight is not victory, the dream is laziness, only action can sate the soul and save the world. I experienced the whole odyssey of searching and agitation but now, look, the work of art rises unwavering, like an island on the heaving open sea, and I have anchored, I trust, in the good harbor with the ancestral olive tree.

Arpagos slowly raised his head. The holy procession of stars had silently begun to climb and traverse the heavens, and the River Jordan, in ferment, was spilling across the sky from end to end. He smiled at the awesome nightly wonder, and as he lowered his eyes to his friends he felt a sweetness rising from his entrails, a feeling of compassion and charity and ineffable humility.

—Myros, he exhorted his third friend, you, too, must raise your glass and chide me.

—You know, Arpagos, answered Myros, with that profound grieving voice of his, you know better than I the rhythm of God's footsteps: He continuously shatters every harmony, constantly yearning for what is loftier. Kosmas wrestles in the cursed field of men, to harmonize his idea with action and prod the sluggish mule of earth to fall in step with his quick pulse. Petros struggles with a more dangerous and recalcitrant enemy: words—the wild mares of Mount Parnassos that slip between man's fingers, all spirit and gallop. I, too, struggled with man and with the word, but they could not contain my agitation and hope—all these matrices burst and the great sperm crushes my heart. I look at the greatest men around me: They're all building the pillar of God, carving his feet, decorating the base; a few are climbing on his knee, attending to his breast. But I should like to stand on the divine shoulders and capture and forge the tranquil majestic countenance in bronze, unmoving, loftier than the ephemeral waverings of the heart. But myriad gods of soft mud, my slaves, with countless faces, are born and die between my ten burning fingers. And I don't want them—I seek a God unmoving, superior to me, eternal. *Ah!* I scream, but can say nothing more. I hide, I strain, I want to break out of my sheath, to be saved from man, to leap out like a sword. The sheathed butterfly screams the same *ah!* as spring approaches, and thrills and struggles to tear through, straining in a mysterious contest for its prize. And every moment God screams the same *ah!*

But your eyes shine calmly, Arpagos, like two deep springs. I sense that you stand 'in the presence of The Presence' and reflect the glow of the Invisible's countenance. You remember, since childhood we went to school and roamed the streets together, loved the same women, longed for the same summits, and how many countless times we slept on the same pillow. And now . . . I acknowledge and rejoice in the harsh hand of God. Who said He holds a scale and, like a good father, divides the bread equally among his children? I gave my blood, I screamed at night, I roamed the whole earth knocking on God's door, crying: 'Open, I am man! I am not an ant for you to step on! I am man, the same as you in desire and hope. Open!' But no one answered. And you, sitting quietly by the seashore talking with the fishermen and playing with your dog, one night, without expecting him, you welcomed this Great Traveler on your threshold. Yes, God comes like Death, without our knowing the hour or moment.

Open your heart, Arpagos, and help us!

II
ARPAGOS

—BELOVED FRIENDS, lovely indeed is this nocturnal eve, and ineffable the starlit holy awe above us; our hearts kick like infants within these earthen breasts of ours, and knowingly or not, like good shepherds bent over our crooks, we all contemplate the brimming invisible presence in the manger of God.

Our dinner tonight is truly like a mystical symposium to me. And like the Noblemen of old I should have liked to present each of you, dear friends, with a dinner gift: To you, Myros, a pearl, large and precious like a tear, to remember me by. And to Petros, a gold cup, etched with the great journey of Dionysos of India—who set out clothed in multicolored tunics, bedecked with ornaments, relics, and perfumes; who grew embarrassed as he ap-

proached and breathed the light air of Greece, and
threw away the superfluous vain load, and set foot
on the holy soil dressed only in his nudity, glowing
like a god. And to Kosmas, I'd give a serving maid,
skillful at the loom and in bed; so that when he
returned to his room, tired and shamed by men, he
could look upon a simple, tender-as-a-doe woman,
sitting cross-legged in the corner who, by her existence, would justify and ease his life. But I am a poor
Nobleman, and instead of gifts, I am overwhelmed
by a terrible desire to follow the mystery of confession.

I know that each person transubstantiates his
temporal life in his own particular way; however, it
is good to confess our struggle, to expose the method
of our own soul, and to take aim at our new hope. In
this way similar souls will shorten their agony and
others will attempt to find their own liberation with
even stronger determination. But all together, unbe-
knownst to all, with exercise, with transient and ever
more difficult victories, with renewed hopes, willing
or not, they ascend the Mountain of God.

You reproached me, Kosmas, and yet, without
your knowing it, our two spirits walk in the same
rhythm; but I fought as best I could, widening the circle of my vision, conquering my individual vicissi-
tude, to breathe the acrid air of God.

And I shall sing your praises, Kosmas, before I start my confession, because I know that you have stood on the first rung of initiation. But the ascent that you did not complete I tried with prodigious struggle to surpass.

But before all others, it is righteous to remember the One, as we spill three drops of wine on the dry fine sand:

Lord, if I raise my head, I shall see you standing before me smiling, with your finger at your mouth,

but I hold you and breathe you and am in no hurry.

With bowed head, with eyes and mouth closed, I rejoice in your descent.

You descend like the great river of Misiriou[1] from secret high sources, heavy, dense, full of semen, without roar and urgency,

and the date palms are the first to perceive you from afar, and their swordlike peaks glow, and their branches flutter excitedly as they proclaim the great message down to the arid sand

and all the roots thirstily crumble the soil, eager to hear if indeed you are approaching

and all the small creatures, locusts and scarabs, sniff the moist air and exult, and the calves abandon the nipple and leap ecstatically, without knowing why.

All the earth quivers like a woman in the bridal chamber, with her eye on the closed door.

And you descend without noise and urgency, red as blood, steaming like heavy must, from plethoric begetting,

and whatever you touch becomes a mouth and drinks of you and grows bigger and the soil swells and fills with worms and plants and camels and people.

And whatever you don't touch remains fallow, cursed, and unsowed, like the womb of a marble woman and the unviolated she-goat.

Lord, Lord, I lifted myself up like a palm tree on the edge of your path so you could nourish me.

I shall raise you to my peak, with all my roots, so you can see and delight in your works.

And I shall place my heart on the uppermost branch with head turned upward toward the light, to warble for your pleasure,

to warble like the nightingale that collapses, with bloodied beak from excess song.

Kosmas, your lean body rose often before me here in my solitude, and I felt you collaborating in my secret struggle. Many a time I went out sleepless in the dark, and looked down toward the sea and called your name. I knew you, too, were sleepless, and crying out. I could see your lamp glowing in the night of Hellas, like a star.

They were all bowed down like slaves, breathing the polluted air of the herd, yoked to the winch of a cheaply valued life. You, alone, were not easily accommodated; compromises did not go well with your lofty nature and, one day, ignoring the prudent smiles, you said: I will save Greece.

But the abstract idea of Country did not satisfy your carnivorous spirit. You wanted to touch Greece bodily, to drink from all her springs, to tread her mountains and citadels, to size up the Romaic spirits[2] on her islands, in Rumeli,[3] and high up in the Balkans and beyond, deep in Anatolia.

Whenever you surveyed a peak your spirit stirred; and you climbed it, shivering, to delight in the sight of the slender body of Greece as she emerged from the dark blue waters and basked in the sun.

You went from village to village, amid sickness and wretchedness, prodding everything around you to aspire and to work. And like the golden green beetle with the stark yellow belly that pounces on all the flowers in the garden, you fluttered your wings and settled on the barren Greek hearts, and with patience and rage and love you awakened within them the cry of the Romaic fate.

'I will save Greece,' you reflected, means 'I will

save my soul.' You burned for your own perfection, inflamed by the all-sacrificing and persevering love of the Race. You closed your eyes and felt the Tribe's voice welling up in you like a spring, and your being merging mystically, as one—like the blossom on the tree—with the Romaic sea, with the mountains and the people, dead and alive and unborn. And there was something deeper still, inexpressible and secret, which was rising to your eyes like the 'compassionate tear' of the great ascetics.

Whenever you said 'I,' all Hellas took on consciousness, her soil and waters, the people, the past and the future, and they spoke with your mouth. Wherever you sensed a Romaic heart growing faint and ebbing away, you rushed over as though a member of your own body were in danger and you kindled the blood and roused the mind and you gathered the small children in the midst of danger and taught them to sing the 'Anthem.'

I liked you, Kosmas, and from this cliff I admired you, scouting in the air like a hawk, and swooping down raucously on the Romaic soul in its last gasp at Aivali,[4] or Proussa[5] or up in Kastoria.[6]

At this hour, Joachim,[7] in this brilliant starlit night when I have before me this young man whom you so loved, it is you I am thinking of, Joachim.

On foot, with your sack over your shoulder, impervious to climate and men, exiled from the Throne of the Universe for thirteen years, you traversed the ascetic roads of Mount Athos and rattled on doors from Monastery to Monastery, like a humble peddler monk; but in your mind you were weaving the gold, weighted-down vestments with the black eagles, and quietly putting *Kampayia*[8] on your feet.

Because you disdained solitude and did not comprehend it; the boundaries of meditation were narrow and you felt stifled; paper did not give forth blood to quench your eagle-heart's thirst, and life had no value without men for you to govern. You were not hunting in the eternal spring plain of fantasy for intellectual butterflies, fleshless and soundless, with only light and color and rhythm—you were a hunter of men. And like Draco of Greek mythology, in wordless quest you'd twitch your nostrils at the scent of human flesh. You were always hungry, oh, Giant, and the fatted calf with the swordlike horns was more welcome to you than the hymn.

You had no doubts, because like a good shepherd your will raised everything to your own footpath. You believed in God and in yourself; nothing existed outside you two.

You still hover high over the *Polis*[9] like a two-headed eagle and you hold it in your talons like a lamb and don't want it to get away. Cradled beneath the marbled pillow, with the embroidered symbols of the Empire, the keys of Aghia Sophia[10] lie gleaming, always ready, and one day, oh, Bishop of the Greeks, you will rise and go of your own volition to celebrate the Divine Liturgy.

Who can stand up to your voice? *Lift up . . . O gates!*[11] The gold mosaics will burst over them, bouncing off the plaster shroud, and the triumphant paean of the Commandress will ring out: 'To thee, champion Leader . . . thank-offering of victory . . .'[12] and the crystal chandeliers will all light up at once, and the wild dove will again stand at the pulpit, balancing its two wings.

Oh, *Akrita*,[13] you brandish your golden bishop's staff like an *apelatiki*,[14] and the heavens' armies— Angels, Archangels, Thrones, Sovereigns, Powers, Rulers, Cherubim, and Seraphim—all around you, Commander, await the Signal.

And you keep silent and breathe, fighting inside the stone cocoon of posthumous metamorphosis. And as you breathe, the frontiers of Hellas creak and break because you are the *Genos*[15]—something broader and deeper than narrow Hellas, our rich, troubled, multispermed Anatolian *Genos*, full of people, gods, and monsters—the indestructible *Genos of Romiosini!*[16]

The three friends were silent. They shivered as though the great shadow had passed over them.

In time Kosmas said:

—You resurrected the indomitable father before my eyes, Arpagos. And I felt his heavy hand on top of my head again, blessing me—as though he were ploughing me.

It was night—I had gone to the Polis hurriedly to get his blessing. I raced through the narrow streets of Phanariou, eyeing the Polis greedily, left and right, and saying to my heart: 'Hold steady, old heart— she'll be yours!'

I was to leave the next morning for distant mountains, to start a school right in the Bulgarian camp and I didn't know if I'd get there alive. So I was hurrying to receive communion from the Commander's strength. The Patriarch eyed me evenly, taking aim, as though he were weighing me. It was the first time he had seen me. Suddenly, extending his hand, he placed it on my head and said: 'A teacher in Kastoria last year, a twenty-five-year-old Hellene, didn't have the courage to take the children to church on the 25th of March.[17] A Bulgarian teacher took a bomb that same day and went right into our Consulate—into a whole crowd of frightened Greeks who had timidly started to sing, "I know you from your dreadful cutting edge . . ."[18] and flung the bomb on the table. They tore him to pieces, but not a word of complaint came out of his mouth, and he glowed all over from head to toe. Now those are the kind of teachers our Race needs.'

—And you were throwing bombs, too, Kosmas. You played life like a dangerous delightful game, disdaining men's existence as a mere detail, quietly and persistently aiming at one thing only—the integral Obligation.

Whenever you passed through Athens—always in a hurry—you loathed the certainty of life there, you couldn't fit into their homes and you fled, taking the young men with you to some deserted country chapel, and there you would speak to them. And the snowcovered Macedonian mountains,[19] Peristeri, Holomondas, Pangaio, Beles, would rise in their young imaginations, and the murky waters of Strimonas and Vardaris[20] would flow thick and rich like royal veins.

And the villages would appear in the distance, among the fir trees, or down in the muddy plains, where they were waiting for the "Hellenes" to come and swiftly strike the Greek bells in the churchyard and call upon the God of Hellas to finally take up arms and begin!

The youths listened to the lisping, stuttering, Moses-like voice of yours, and the smell of blood stirred their minds and they could no longer stand their mediocrity. You came from legendary places, apostle of danger, a frontier guard who stood erect and fought the barbarians even in the farthest outpost of the land.

At times, awkward and Bacchus-like, you softly hummed Anatolian tunes to them, or tunes from Epiros or Macedonia, and the wild rhythm grabbed the youthful bodies, like a distant woman's erotic song. And sometimes you'd get up and all of you together would weave a dance—polemic, erotic, and barbaric. You poured new blood, like potent unfiltered wine, into the Hellenistic veins, and their pining life glinted suddenly on their breast, like a knife.

Efthini[21], the tenth Muse, who never sits still on the lap of man, leaped within you, Kosmas, armed to the teeth, like an unsubdued cry. And you said: It is my Obligation to do whatever no one obliges me to do, to load myself down with every sin, and to grow where no one has sown me.

Remember what you wrote me one day when you were agonizing, wounded, in an Epiros cellar: 'I am the goat of the Old Testament, loaded down on both sides with the sins of a whole people, heading toward the wilderness to get killed.'

But I fear, continued Arpagos, laughing, that my praise of Kosmas is almost spilling over the holy boundaries of its purpose. And, furthermore, I forget that in the hand of Xeniou Dia[22], the wine cup should never remain empty.

Smiling, Helen rose and filled the glasses. They began to drink slowly, and the countenance of the men floated in the wine, vast, clear and sober, as though the mystical drink had suddenly, here in this deserted seashore, rediscovered its integral meaning.

—I prefer the goat of the ancient dance, said Petros. Behind his beastly mask, he protected the eternal man. He received the blood of God in Holy Communion, he merged and became one with him, and for one supreme moment he lived his joys and his loss. And later, when the sacred Orgy was over, he set the furry goatskin and the wedge-shaped beard, the footgear and the thyrsus on the altar and once again became a simple man. And he returned to his home, relieved of his passions because he had been relieved of God's passions, and tranquilly went on with the drudgery of life. The vision had mellowed the soul and held it steady over the black chaos.

—And isn't the goat, said Myros, smiling, that a simple man eats at night with his wife and children, that becomes blood and human flesh and desire and thought and hope, isn't this, too, a holy communion, a transubstantiation, full of mystery and awe?

—In the highest circle of divinity, said Arpagos, there is no such thing as small and large, preference and condemnation, nature or miracle. Everyone, stooped over the great Ocean, takes as much of the Ocean as he can hold in his cupped hand; but even in the tiniest drop, the initiate's eye delights in the whole God, without shoreline, without bottom, without beginning, without end, one and incalculable that only the heart of man can contain.

An old peasant once told me, as we were sitting before the fire on a winter's eve in Mani,[23] sharing the flame of the divine countenance: 'In the days of our grandfathers, when God used to come down to earth, he said to Man one day: "The seven tiers of heaven and the seven tiers of earth cannot contain me; but the heart of man can contain me. Take care not to wound the heart of even the humblest man because I may be in there." '

The eye of the initiate can ferret out whole the vision of God even in the humblest worm. I'll never forget a dream I had one night: A tiny bug like a black bee, completely covered with huge bluish-black antennas, sat motionless on the soil; and right in the center of it were two tiny jet black eyes that shone deeply, grievous and tender. A divine fear swept over me and, like Moses before the burning bush, I stood there and shuddered. 'It's God!' I said, and when I woke up in terror my pillow was soaked with tears.

My beloved Kosmas, this is how I saw the spark

that was consuming you inside. And I thought: in word and in deed, an order superior to you, which you do not embrace, works and stretches upward. You want to exorcise the ennui of life with danger. You think that your tribe and the mountains and islands become obedient stepping stones for your soul to climb and, from the chilling peak of surveillance, look upon the futile, as you say, fate of man. And you don't understand that it is not in your power to escape. You serve an end superior to you.

—What end? Our mind has matured and no longer worships any master. I know that life is a spark that shines for a moment between two endless nights. But I want, out of pride, not out of hope, to hold my body straight and let the holy spark at my head consume and melt it. Relentless battle is needed always, clamor and action, so that we do not hear the secret voice that cries inside the folds of our heart, quietly, like the monotonous, silent rain. All is futile and only action, like wine, deceives and uplifts us somewhat.

Like the brave sailor who works night and day at the pump on his leaky ship, while the others all fold their hands and curse or cry or raise their eyes toward heaven, as the water continues to rise, a hair every hour; and only he, calmly biting his lip, keeps raising and lowering his arm, working the pump and deeply inhaling the futility—

I, too, suffer, working at this leaky ship of Earth upon which we have embarked.

I disturb you, Arpagos, but we're free, and confession, you know, is a harsh virtue and suits us.

—Silently I take joy in you, Kosmas, that you, too, like it or not, climb the Mountain of God on such an impassable road. Because the essence of divinity is always: the battle to rout matter and subdue our opposing impulses to an obstinate rhythm. Except that you work enslaved, because you have not yet been able to live the integral purpose that your struggle serves; only if you live it will you be liberated, because in living it you make the integral purpose yours.

—Purpose doesn't exist. Hope degrades man and we suckle the milk of valor only through the breast of despair. Do you search for a harbor, Arpagos? Shame on you! Only the dead have found the harbor. We live and cruise the black sea with open mainsails, jibs, and lateens, and we sail overtly toward death.

Arpagos was grieved by his friend's words and fell silent for a while. A fishing boat passed slowly under the light of the stars. Its oars beat in rhythm and a voice rose passionately, singing of woman: *The Earth gnaws at my feet and the wind gnaws at my hair, and a little dark-haired maiden gnaws at my entrails.*

All held their breath, to listen. The song rose clear,

triumphant, like a paean, and the entire boat of work and poverty glowed suddenly like the pearly shell bearing the emerging Aphrodite.

—Ah! Song! shouted Petros. The essence of the world, the voice of immortality that the small, transient gods of our mind vainly try to strangle!

—I, too, exclaimed Myros, am flooded with compassion for the young man who aches, for myself, for everything on Earth. Eternal sorrows and joys awaken in me, complete erotic love, full of mud, blood, and vertigo.

Suddenly Arpagos raised his voice:

—Here, my silence breaks abruptly. I am no longer concerned with friendships. My heart barks like a bitch guarding her master's vineyard!

You came to my solitude, Kosmas, bearing Episcopacy[24] like a great new goddess. You took her ready-made from the bazaars of *Frankia*[25] and you bring her to Greece: 'Everything is a futile and ephemeral plaything of the eyes. And only one Eye inside us, ephemeral, too, but clear and unmerciful, never blurred by suffering, surveys the spectacle of life from on high. A Theater, where we have a view and see, and at the same time are in the scene, performing. Viewers and actors. Indeed, the more we perform the more tragic the spectacle becomes, and more pleasurable, because we sprinkle it with aware-ness, with harshness, with our heart's blood.

'Out of all the delusions we select one, the one which matches us best, and we proclaim it the Truth. We raise its banner high, shouting, working, killing; but inside us, in our uppermost being, unparticipat-ing, mocking, cold, aware of the ruse, the Eye follows the futile and picturesque intoxication, inside the lumination of death.'

Behold your labors' reflections, behold what makes you defy danger and love life. Like some birds I'm ashamed to name, you stir up a storm around you with motions of creativity; without phallus, without womb, without sperm.

And you, Petros, came to my solitude carrying your beautiful songs and harsh questions. Once, in-toxicated from divine wine, you wrote me: 'I con-quered futility, I compelled matter to become eternal, I found the immortal water, by creating. The world was made, it struggles, it laughs and cries, wars break out, empires fall, man whispers intimacies to woman, Death blows and strips the tree of Earth bare—all this so the Poet can see and rescue it with song. All the world is a Troy, burning for the sake of Homer. Thousands of suitors followed Helen as she played and fluttered in the sun, like a queen bee. But only one, the divine Drone, the Poet, made her his in eter-nity!'

I didn't answer you then, knowing well that only the warm air of illusion could make you struggle unflaggingly and ripen the seed that God entrusted to you. But now, this is what I answer you:

I met an old monk in a cave one day, at a cloister on Mount Athos. I stayed with him and at night, after vespers, as we were sitting outside the tiny grave-filled courtyard, I listened to the adventures of his soul: 'I was a gendarme,' he said, 'chasing a fugitive in the mountains of Rumeli near Chrisos. I drank and I pillaged and was a terror wherever I went, like a brigand. One Saturday night I arrived at a small hamlet and went to the priest's house for lodging. I had just received a letter from my village—my wife had died years ago and now, the only child I had in this world, the light of my life, my little Dimitri, had fallen sick and died. So I was speechless and when I got to the priest's house and had eaten a crust of bread I stretched out on the sofa to sleep. But how could I sleep! The priest's little girl in the corner of the room had lit the lantern and was reciting the primer for hours on end. I got angry, cursed and started to get up but, suddenly, I don't know why, I was overcome with weeping. In the morning I went to church just as they were reading the gospel. The words of Christ seemed sweet to me, like honey. I abandoned everything, got into a caique and came out to the wilderness, God be praised!'

Can you give us a song like that, Petros? Can you change the world's tempo like that? Can you separate man's life in two: before he hears your word, and after he hears it. And have it sound sweet like honey to him, or like a thunderbolt as it did to Saul? Not a mere fancy hors d'oeuvre; nor something to whet the human palate for just a minute. But wheatbread that nourishes the bones.

And if you can't do this, what do I care about your work? In other ages when faith nourished souls, the decorative tributes at God's feet were good, and good, too, the angels and ascetics or youthful horsemen on the pediments, and good the song that praised virtue and woman and the other small hopes of Earth. And good the peacock of beauty, with the spreading multimeshed wings at the feet of the Most High. But now we are floundering, God is missing, souls are dying of hunger!

Led astray by Frankish concerns yourself, you eulogize woman, shrieking like an ailing man, or you sing of weariness, grief, ennui, and now, swayed by the winds of Frankish Europe, you warm over the dead gods.

But the Franks are gone: Their gods fell and shattered to pieces.

Lord! Lord! Who despised Frankdom more than I—with its worship of logic and the belly, with its miserable knowledge and its expedient little certainties?

Who rejoices and dances because Frankdom is gone; thousands of cartloads of those infidels were killed and now, look, supreme Responsibility is again in Anatolia, on our soil, to give new meaning to life and new passionate Hope!

Shout for joy, daughter of War! You surge from God's brain armed to the teeth and purify the earth through devastation!

Where are you, Lord? I don't want you with an evangelical lily in your hand, but with a sword! Enough of mercy and goodness. The world has rotted to its roots, and you must plant a new one. And if five righteous men, or even ten, must be lost, don't take pity on them. Bind your head tightly with your kerchief so that your mind doesn't waver, and strike!

They took your throne, they opened pits for you to fall in, they polluted the hearth and snuffed out your divine fire—how can you still bear them in the palm of your hand, Lord, and give them the sun and the rain and male children?

Inside this earthen Romaic heart of mine I feel a new civilization, clear and simple, and every day I struggle on this steep rock, far from the Frankish hearts that have rotted, to distinguish and grasp the new countenance of supreme Hope.

Once, faint from anguish, I remember you telling me, Myros: 'It's all over with Greece, she's lost, her strength has ebbed, her blood is watered down, she can no longer conceive and give birth to the hero. So why should she continue to live? Let her die!'

But I, in the stillness of the night, listened. And two, three, ten voices, from the far ends of Romiosini[26] were answering.

One was saying: 'Hellas is not geography and memory. She is not you and me nor is she the thousands of Greeks who pollute her. She lives and reigns inside me, indestructible, and she has the boundaries of my soul and her capital is the Polis in me.'

And someone from the other end was speaking softly: 'I feel inside me a new light, a new order, a new color, a different rhythm, a spirited song like an Anatolian fairy tale, wealth and power that don't belong to me, but to Hellas. She is inside me like a seed and kicks and doesn't let me sleep.'

And a third voice, a woman's, was rising from the depths of the earth and was saying: 'My breasts are veined with the milk of valor. Grant, oh, God, that I bear a Son who will enter the Polis.'

And harshly, then, I turned to myself and said: 'And you, what have you to say? What do you seek?'

I seek, I replied, and the sweat of my agony ran over all my body, I seek to find the heart, the beginning and end, the purpose of Hellas, where every voice will find and take its place, that not a drop of strength and grace be lost. I seek the essence of the struggle—God.

—You seek a new religion? said Kosmas, ironically, with a laugh.

—I don't know, my friend, and I'm not concerned with naming my struggle and the method of my liberation with words. I seek a place where I can stand sure-footed, where you, too, can stand. I seek to find the source of my life, that is, of universal life, and the justification of endeavor. Call it Religion, God, Chimera, Song, Delusion—what do I care? I call it Liberation.

Myros could not hold back the tears. The hapless athlete's sobbing sounded in the evening's darkness.

—Arpagos, he said, trying to subdue his emotion, you promised us the formidable pursuit of the mystery of confession. But so far, you've only sung the praises of Kosmas, with such love that it struck us as harsh—because I am well aware that the hand of love is one with the hand of God: It always demands more than we can give and it breaks our clutching fists because it gives more than they can hold.

And then you shattered Petros' song, blowing the breath of God on it; and me, you pitied, and didn't voice your contempt for my sterile training and my empty hands.

Now, keep your word, reveal your struggle, show us the road to your liberation, help us rise to the peak of our strength, too.

Like the busy barren bee, I was locked in my heart, with folded wings, hungry and trembling; forging all night with my most precious substance the enormous royal cradles that would hold the divine scion; and all around them I welded together the countless humble honeycombs of the barren populace. And the whole human beehive appeared like the legendary Delphic temple of Apollo, made up entirely of wax and feathers.

And I trembled because the flowers were wilting and the sun was filling with clouds and the marriage was late in coming.

But, just as the queen bee suddenly descends in the midday heat from her white flaming height with the lance of love still plunged in her full belly, and the bees swoop down on her downy convulsing body, inhaling the salvation,

I, too, Arpagos, search your hands, your hair, your mind, your silence and your speech, and I smell the erotic thunderbolt of God on you, like brimstone.

III
ARPAGOS

I BEGIN THE CONFESSION. I shall speak without apparent order, simply following the inner rhythm that impels me. I shall fight to force my blood to remember the fierce battle, breaking the rigid crust of logic, laziness, and habit that hides my soul.

A savage cry might escape me now and then, or tears or laughter or scorn, and on occasion I may remain silent; I know quite often I shall have to force myself to keep from leaping up and dancing, or sinking to the floor and giving in to despair.

I shall let my heart scream, because I am not creating art. Because in a few hours I shall distill my life, all my horror and joy, my love, shame, agony, and redemption. Because I want to renew with you tonight a confession like that of the first Christians who fell trembling to the floor of the church, declaring their sins to everyone before receiving holy communion.

When I veer suddenly, stopping the flux of life, and am able to distinguish what is behind me, I shudder at the sight of my ancient sins, the agony and toil before I was born, of the race which is full of gnarls, villainy, and spite . . .

The only Muse of my race was Necessity, who is forever hungry, thirsty, and cold. She seizes the deer by the foot on the run. She stoops, rustles the sticks of wood, and lights the fire. She diffuses the water's dewiness in the air and ploughs the soil with her nails and, look, the water bounces on the soil as though from a breast, and she suckles the earth. Necessity looks at woman and says: I want her. She looks at man, desires him, and whispers: Sleep with me . . .

And the race multiplies—hearths, cradles, shepherd's crooks, bows, clamor. Smoke emerges from rooftops, huts rise and take over the slope. They spread and dig in along the river. And in the center stands the Old Progenitress, tall, with double breasts, long nails, conches and bones in her hair, smeared with grease and painted with saffron. She gathers the young men and girls in the caves and lets out a savage cry, like war and like love. *Aaa* . . . And the feet ignite, the eyes grow blurred, they grasp each other by the hands, by the waist, by the shoulders, and they leap and dance and let out piercing shrieks. And one of them threads bow strings through the skull of a horse and starts a monotonous, wild, melancholy tune—and the feet pick up the rhythm and all beat the ground together and speak to the earth. The conches reverberate on the shoulders, and a young girl swoons. And suddenly a youth leaves the dance and stands in the center and begins the tune: 'Bring out the mare, I bid you farewell! I shall cross the river; I shall go to the village of our enemies; I shall burn their tents and crops, and I shall seize the chief's only daughter, Darampa, from his hearth.'

I can still feel a barbaric, all-hairy bellow and mud inside me. As I wander through the cities and look at the houses, the women, the silks, books, lights, I grow edgy and savage, as though I'm seeing them for the first time. My brain feels thick like the swollen field in the rain. I feel a god neighing in my bowels, who is like me, archaic—all hairiness, bellow, and mud. And he screams, remembering his old hungers: 'I came because your cellars are full and we are hungry, because your houses are big and empty and I have no place to put my children, because your women wear gold earrings and mine have grown jealous and begin to complain—and I crossed the river and came and I shall fill their aprons with ears and with earrings!'

I remember one night when I was walking alone, on a very high mountain. Never had I so enjoyed such a brilliant enormous moon above the snow. Below, very deep in a ravine, the lights of a tiny town flickered playfully. I was walking quietly, beguiled by the solitude, the silence, and the moon. And suddenly, unconsciously, I clenched my fists. I turned abruptly toward the town and muttered through set teeth: I will burn you all!

As soon as I said this, I came to, and unbearable shame overwhelmed me.

Ah! The blood never forgets, it roars inside us like a river, all slime, carnage, and sperm, and when it finds our limited conscience off guard, not watching the fence, it breaks through and leaps up to the lips and eyes, with clamor and desire. And suddenly, in a lightning flash, we look back into the thousands of years, and shudder. Our contemporary, impoverished, wretched soul, all-wary, logical, and compromising is a thin skin that struggles to cover and drown, deep within us, fierce primordial forces. But these lightning flashes come, sleep comes, the Prophet comes, and breaks the skin and frees them!

As a child I often felt this skin stirring from the explosion within, and cracking. The world, like a dense vision, seemed to be one with me—the stars touched me, the sea broke over my brain and refreshed it. I remember as an infant the first time I crawled to the threshold and leaned out into our little garden: It was noon, all the air was humming, huge bees like angels were going about talking to the flowers, and dizziness overtook me, full of buzzing, fragrance, light, bustle.

And when I first began to walk and started, as best I could, to put order into the chaos, and to narrow down the world, the air filled with invisible enemies—angels and demons and voices in the night. The first terrifying Siren took me and sat me on her knees. Late each afternoon I'd return from my tutor—oh, how I'd leaf through the old biographies of the saints, barely able to read, and plunge myself in the wilderness!

Never in my later life did I live my own pain so agonizingly as I lived and suffered the martyrdom of the saints as a child. I plunged into the hippodromes, I was devoured, screaming, by wild beasts, I was tied to the wheels, I climbed the pyre, I was stoned, I was crucified, I fasted, I saw the angels protecting me, I perceived God in my heart like the knife of slaughter. My soul breathed in an air of madness, blazing, full of incense, light and blood. I remember hurrying along the street one day, the tears still fresh from my crying over the life of John the Kalibite. 'My God, if you'd only make me God!' I said suddenly.

But as soon as the words escaped, I realized my sin and reproached myself bitterly. I confessed to no one, but that night, secretly from my parents, I put nails next to my flesh and went to sleep.

I remember only two joys in the gloom of my childhood life:

a dark-skinned peddler from Egypt, who made the rounds selling dates, manna, Indian nuts, perfumes and necklaces—scenting the air wherever he passed,

and a tall, fair woman in our neighborhood who used to sit me, a child of three, on her knees, and I would lean on her warm breast and smell her bosom with inexpressible giddiness. And even now, after forty years, I quiver remembering that joy; never since then have I felt so deeply the mystery of the female bosom, that is full of milk, delight, and holiness.

As I grew older, my misery and wretchedness increased. Like a winding ball of vipers it slithered inside me, unfolding sins: falsehood, fear, cruelty, muddy, unclean desires, without name or face, like chaos. The cell that fate gave me to work in was all mud and gore. My ancestors were grasping, working as hirelings, eating barley bread, and their brain was full of earth. But a flame without meaning and purpose was burning them. I took on all their virtues and evils and felt them fighting inside me. I took all their unfulfilled desires—the sins they never dared commit, the women they were never able to kiss, dark hatred and passion, and even their stifled, indestructible yearning to escape the beast working in them.

Ever since I was a small child, the forces of good and evil, with centuries-old roots, struggled fiercely within me.

The moment I'd begin, fearfully, to tell a lie, I would suddenly hear voices rise inside me:

'I loathe being stuck with you. I want to flee, to be free of you. Uncouth impulses, shame, passion, and fear govern you at bottom. You wallow in animal mire up to your neck and I want to escape, to breathe clean air. You suffocate me! I want freedom!

'I'm filled with vulgarity and slime. I hate my superiors, I fear those stronger than me, I ridicule whatever I cannot attain, I torment the weak. But I feel a flame pass through my heart and flicker over my head. I am the extinguished, heavy ancestral candle that caught fire. I'll burn in order to nourish the flame at my head. From the depths of evil the Savior ascends. Don't laugh!'

'What Savior?'

'You!'

Oh, mystical unity, muddy current, curdled with blood and sludge and gold, where I swim, straining to keep my head up, and my mouth closed!

Oh, Heracles, megalomartyr athlete, weighed

down by massive flesh, full of mud and crimes, laboring below your worth, but rising always from exploit to exploit, to lighten and become god.

And in school when the teachers were trying to explain the ancient tragedies to me, God, how I'd smash the words, and how the creative breath would pour out whole, without obstructions, without substance, and would become one with my own joys and sorrows! Life eternal was in those verses, joyful and despairing—water and fire, crone and maiden and infant, elusive, merciless, thousand-countenanced and free!

And, lo, from within the word, as though from a tomb, like a dry branch unfolding, Helen would come forth and walk on earth once more, on the warm soil, slender, silent, swaying like a palm tree. And Electra, like a bony bloodhound, would come skipping behind her, barefoot, flat-bosomed, with enormous eyes that looked eternally beyond, toward the dusty road . . .

One morning as I was walking down an island seashore I saw a huge lump of clay being kneaded by the idle sunburnt hands of a laborer; and I saw it rise suddenly and dance on the whetstone, overcoming its heavy nature and taking on all the marvels of gyration, as though it were spirit, as though it were a ringlet of fire—

this is the kind of hand I was beginning to feel inside me, crushing me—and what a holy dance!

From then on two voices began to consciously battle within me. Like a man and a woman.

The one would shout: I want freedom! I am the arrow that wants to break the woof and warp, to fly out of the loom of necessity.

To break through nature, to overcome the law, to renounce my father and my mother—

I am illusion, the door of besieged life, the essence of the male phallus!

The other voice would resist and reply: I sit cross-legged on the soil, I spread my roots deep into the tombs, I accept the sperm and sit motionless in order to nurture it. I am all weight and nourishment and necessity

and I want to turn back, to regress to the animal, to fall back to the vegetative, and not stir. I've become weary. I hate life, power, hope, the flame that ascends

and I fight, using diverse pleasure to smother the male.

> *Ah! what is this good, that I cannot rise from sheer sweetness of the air!**

*See Chapter 1, Note 3

I still tremble remembering the endless, murky years of puberty, full of mystery, horror, and sweetness. Everything touched me with a multifaceted harsh eroticism. The sun filled my clenched hands and settled in them like a golden ball; the first rains of autumn beat against my face and I shivered all over with pleasure and dread.

Lord, what should I remember first? The Great Wind on Mount Parnassos, the divine morning that followed, the waterfalls on the slopes, a barefoot shepherdess about twelve years old, sunburned and silent, leaning on a long staff; how she smiled when I bid her good morning; her whole face lit up at once and glowed. And I thought: Lord, how you shone on this dark countenance! You gleamed, your teeth sparkled snowy-white from barley bread, your cheeks blazed in the crystal air, your little shepherd's staff swayed like thyrsus, and your entire little girlish heart gave itself to the wayfarer, like a woman!

Remember the deaf lightning that passed over the peaks of the olive trees one night and fell on the autumnal earth, and how she received it tremblingly, as though it were the ravaging glance of the Descending God who is ready to transubstantiate himself into erotic rain and merge with Demeter on the plowed field

and the blooming lemon trees one Easter at

Mistra,[1] where you were walking, Arpagos, weak and faint from the aroma and from an unforeseen grief, when you suddenly leaned against a tree and began to cry and rant.

I would cry without reason. I'd roam the fields, and when I'd see a woman I would seethe with indignation and turn away. In the morning I'd get up tired and silent. Even if everyone falls in the trap, I'd say to myself, out of disgust and pride I will not fall. Life grabs man and woman without mercy and unites them like two loads of flesh in order to meet its aims. But my eyes are open, I see the shame and forgive nothing!

And I'd say: You must leap, my soul, you must run, you must cast the spear, you must burn and be silent, indomitably hoisting your mind above the female caress.

And so, quietly, unconsciously, the labors of the ascetics ripened and dangled in my mind like fruit. My childhood thirst for martyrdom returned again, firmer and more nubile. And all the springtime agitation of adolescence, instead of ripening the sweet fruit of delight, took a harsh implacable mien within me.

One evening, as I was returning from a dull theater performance, I came across a prostitute on a corner;

gold spangles on her hair and bosom glittered fleetingly, and her every movement glowed in the darkness. I jumped as though I had encountered a snake.

I went home but couldn't sleep. Toward dawn, my eyes still open, I began to experience an intense sensation, as though I were in some incorporeal contact with a hazy picture that was shimmering in the air; Christ, slender and sorrowful, was sitting before an arched low door, and at his feet, quiet, pale, and happy sat Mary looking beyond at the sunny green plain, at the Jordan with the tall reeds, and the sun that was setting. Suddenly, Christ moved a bit and the entire vision sank in a flash, and disappeared.

But my soul, upright, serene, held resolution in her hands, like a ripe apple.

I remember; always when I'm in the throes of battle, I fight, I despair, and cry out; but when, at last, the hour approaches for me to pluck the fruit of disciplined exercise, sweetness pervades my heart, silence and rest. And gently, without effort, at times in a vision, at times in my sleep or when I'm walking along the street unawares, I receive deliverance.

The tree battles in the same way, in secret indestructible conflict, with torrential rains, with cold, with gales, and quietly one noon, in the mild spring sunshine, it emerges in full bloom.

The crisis of adolescence was solved by my fleeing from the world. 'A retreat of the alone toward the alone.'[2]

I left for Mount Athos. I renewed the past retreats of the ascetics.

I went to silence my heart, to see the desert in bloom, so that I, too, might be able to welcome the Lord on my threshold at night. The mind's questions and curses were starting to agitate me. I wanted to win over logic and to take a step beyond that which was certain. I wanted to kill, I said, the mother of all evil—nature. I, too, wanted to gamble the narrow worldly life, the certain life, that could not contain me, in order to win uncertain eternity.

I fled because I was burning with undisciplined fires inside me, with unspeakable eroticisms—toward woman or God, I didn't know—because none of my desires took on a definite face. But I wanted to hold and subdue the natural desires within me, the old legacies, the new passions. It was as though Heracles and the beasts he subdued were one body, wrapped in the same skin and fighting.

I liked danger. I scorned the crumbs I held in my hand and gambled them all to win the Symposium: Do whatever you fear, Arpagos. Break habit, prune your heart, leave only the top of your head to gnaw at the rest of you. Rise, alone, to Stylite. *Ah*, I thought, divine Love and Quiet, the two marvelous forces that assist God in the hour of creation will give all this to me. And these barbaric, veined arms will grow slender, to weightlessly lift the Spirit, like a long-stemmed lily.

Oh! To remain alone, free, far from the wordly grind, outside the corral of the human herd, to be dog, sheep, shepherd, and wolf, and to walk and walk and see nothing but the sun, rain, wind, and stars!

Oh! To feel my entrails like two cloven leaves stirring on the great tree of God! And to give myself to the mistral of the divine breath, gossamery, joyful, dancing and playful—to recreate my life and the world whole, out of my lavish joy.

Askisi,[3] I'd cry, all-powerful goddess, you squeeze your hand like a ripe pomegranate and drain the heart of man,

harsh Mother of Nike,[4] whom you feed with hunger in order to nourish her,

oh, merciless hand, unerring, that leads to deliverance,

like the little year-old blackbird that sits beside the aged blackbird, the way we sit beside a well, and lowers its head at times as if accepting the wise warbling like a blessing, and raises it at other times, thrusting its yellow beak in the buzzing stream of air, trembling —as if on a froth-edged precipice—to plunge into song, similarly, upright before you, oh, *Askisi*, Mother Fountain of unbroken song, I drill my heart to the great hymn of liberation.

Like precious stones freshly emerged dripping from the sea, the cracked Byzantine towers now dance before my eyes . . . the Monasteries amid cypress and lemon trees, the cells in a holy circle surrounding the wide courtyard—and in the center, the great domed cathedral! Stone footpaths stood out white against dense black woods and stopped at the humble convents and deserted chapels. At the seashore a cluster of monks were stooping and pulling in unison at the dragnet brimming with fish, and nearby, a boat that had been dragged onto the crossbar at Arsanas,* had its oars folded across its breast and was sunning itself.

'What a miracle, what solitude, what peace!' I thought, as I climbed.

And as I came up to the first Monastery and set foot on the old sunken threshold, crossing myself as I passed over, a mysterious warmth overtook me. Lord, I cried within me, help me raise my soul higher than joy, happiness, and the multitude,

*A private port or boathouse for each monastery of Mount Athos.

to follow pleasure's loftier hierarchy and to stretch myself up to the eternal Chimera, scorning the earth and her certain riches,

grant that I subdue the body, the heavy sickness of the soul, to break down the door of Hades, to tame the battle, to free myself of small cares, of heavy adornments, of riches and logic, and to be left naked again and immortal, just as I was when you gave birth to me, quietly breathing certainty and erotic love, like the silkworm in its cocoon!

I shivered as I entered the dark church: it was teeming with saints and angels, and there were doves made of stone at the tops of the pillars and magpies and heads of locusts and vines with thick grapes. Trembling, I worshipped at the exquisite miracle-working icon of the *Panaghia Portaitisa*,[5] that angels had carried over the waves while all the sea grew still, kissing the feet of its Mistress in fear,

and I sensed myself surrounded by invisible presences, and Cherubim and Seraphim slid down from the dome and began touching me gropingly.

And the enormous eyes of the *Portaitisa* Virgin, and her round firm chin like Hera's, gleamed sweetly in the darkness.

Glykofilusa,[6] Mistress of the Sea, I said, oh, human Heart who gifted us with Him whom heaven and earth cannot contain. Oh, Deed, who serenely ascends the Mount of Silence and touches the peak of divinity,

oh, Mother, who fructified the rotted tree of life and subdued the miracle, I've come to your garden, I knock on the door of your house, and I am like a closed purple evangelical lily,

like an offering in your hand, Amazon.

Mistress Source, allow me to rest my palms on the shiny stones, to drink the immortal water, so my bones will open like jasmine branches. And to rejoice in my dark countenance, shining sevenfold and motionless in the calm flood of Eternity—

because You are not, I cried, the Mother who only consoles and weeps. The monks in their hymns call you Rose and Apple, Dawn and Cloud, Vine, Shell, Dew, and Nuptial Chamber. But they fall short. What should they name you to reach you, my Mistress? Now they call you Sea, Spa, *Damala*,[7] Portal, Garden, River, Thunder, Tower, Palace, Chalice, and Feast.

But you are the Commandress of my tribe, the Leader of the Hellenic Race, the almighty soul of Romiosini!

At times you are the noble Athenian, in your precious Damascan cloth, highborn from a lordly family; at other times the bold reredos of Rumeli, as though your flesh had hardened in the snows of

Liakoura above Dadi; at other times sweet islander, white sea nymph with a wreath of flowers on your carefully combed and parted hair, and at other times the regal *Korfiatissa*[8] in golden diadem and green silks.

And once in a dream at night you were a Macedonian, with the tall black sheepskin helmet and gold necklaces on your uplifted breast, sunburned, barefoot, in multicolored tatters

and behind you, in a cradle of rope and plane leaves, you were carrying a desolate mountain, your Son.

Oh, Tenth Muse, *Panaghia*,[9] the Crier,

you blazed a cry of danger like a frontier sentry who perceived from afar the swarming Arabs trampling the divine light of Hellas,

and you arose, Commandress, lightly brandishing your *Apelatiki*; and your *yerakokoudouna*[10] and silver *tsaprassia*[11] rang out, and your chaste breast gleamed like the full moon,

and all the young men who were ripe for the twin pleasure of God and Woman leaped up and charged, with you in the lead, oh Amazon,

because you stir in my heart like a Christian Nike who doesn't fear blood and, with long clanging strides, follows the mobilized God on Earth!

As I was speaking, Myros, and looking at the

Portaitisa, I could feel my heart lighten, because the effort I was making to find and express my emotion for the exquisite icon was shedding light on my struggle, and for the first time my inner chaos was becoming distinguishable and taking on a countenance. God, Woman, and War—behold the formidable trinity that was burning me. At times, as I was speaking, I perceived her as a simple and mystical synthesis, an abounding oneness. At other times I could distinguish each brilliant, merciless countenance which hated the others and wanted to capture me whole.

Oh, how I wandered, and with what emotion and urgency, from Monastery to Monastery! I was anxious to choose the harshest of them all to live in—whether for a short while, for long, forever, I didn't know. I felt I had to live alone first, in silence, for months on end. Like a bitch, enduring the confines of house, yard, and garden, fretful and whining, seeking a place to give birth,

I wandered over the Mount, searching.

Now, after so long a time, I close my eyes and thrill at the entire vision:

A Virgin at the edge of the parchment, spinning. She wears the white scarf of a peasant on her head and smiles resignedly; an angel flaps his wing, all-purple on a solid gold background, balancing it with vigor; sleepy-looking martyrs, all peace and bliss, bend over the green Earth as though ready to sleep, and the executioner above slaughters them; and the bloody soil blooms with tiny white daisies and two large lilies.

The capital letters at the beginning of each chapter are embellished with Anatolian richness, weaving with dragons and snakes, with eagles, cypress trees, and birds. I recall a manuscript showing the Holy Spirit descending on the Jordan with the head of a sparrow and a huge wide beak like a pelican's. There are Cherubim and Seraphim with heads of multicolored birds and a jet black Madonna, a negress holding the tiny Christ, ugly, sorrowful and aged, like a dwarf. There is another Madonna with slanted Chinese brows and baggy strabismic eyes.

Farther on, to right and left of the heading, two plumed partridges partially lift their red feet to scratch themselves. Rabbits run about, galleys and caïques travel between the holy writ and books of saints. Palaces, fortresses, armies, kings, and plump babies stand out in rich colors. Flowers growing on a piece of grassy earth beyond gleam like jewels. Dark orange trees are loaded with ruddy fruit, and everything glistens under the flaming breath of the artist.

I see a rendering of the Virgin birth in a Byzantine castle . . . there is the wide bed, the thousand-colored patchquilt, the arched narrow windows separated by tiny double columns and, suddenly—in the midst of the agony of birth, and the ministerings of the midwife who is testing the hot water with her hand—the figure of a woman, the eternal woman, standing before a round mirror, combing her hair.

And farther on, the three Magi. One is an old man, the other is young, and the third is a boy. They are traveling across a gold background on their camels, and as they pass, the dry underbrush blossoms into red flowers as though taking on fire, and a huge star with three rays gleams between heaven and earth, and descends.

I shall never forget the words I read on the old parchment under this painting: As the Magi arrived they were startled to see within the manger that was glowing and changing countenances like a multicolored star—the Saviour. Fear had sealed their mouths, but as soon as they departed with their camels on their homeward trek, they took courage beneath the starry sky at night and spoke:

The first said: *I beheld an infant!*

and the second: *I beheld a man under thirty!*

and the third remained silent for a long time and then said with fear: *I looked upon an ancient man of fathomless years!*

Twelve-year-old Jesus of humble Mount Stavronikita, oh, blooming almond tree in the snow, oh, high and lofty brow, full of understanding, oh, cool night beneath childish eyes, oh, tender breast, holy offering, oh, dismembered Love,

my soul lightened because I remembered you, because for a moment we played again on the green meadow of eternity like two young heifers with stars on our foreheads,

and I thought: I can endure everything because now nothing can ever separate me from you.

And later outside in the open air: a blossoming loquat tree in the Lavras[12] orchard whose scent still makes me swoon, and laurels with their oily berries extending upright for hours, blossoming cherry trees in the ravine, high sandy beaches, and the green anointed sea

and on the threshold of a cloister, a dying old monk whose brain had begun to waver, sitting in the sun beating stones with his iron rod and shouting: "I worked. My hands are full of calluses from penance, my entrails have shrunk from fasting, my skin has become like a turtle's shell from lack of bathing. I never touched a woman, I never wronged anyone, I kept the commandments, I shall enter Paradise!"

And beyond, holy fountains, doves, blackbirds drinking water, conversations with monks . . .

Inside one of the cliffs water was dripping like tears, forming a stagnant mudhole, and as I raised my head to see an icon of the Virgin which was suspended from above, I shuddered. Her cheek was gashed, full of blood.

—A corsair knifed her, whispered a monk who was guarding the house of his Mistress, day and night like a sheepdog. He thought the icon was dead wood and he pulled out his knife, but when he saw the Virgin, all bloody, turning pale and fading, he was struck with terror and fell down screaming, 'Have Mercy, My Lady!' He believed in her grace and the blood stopped. And as her blood stopped, this dry rock immediately began to drip holy water.

—And what do you do here?

—I guard her.

—From what? There are no more pirates. She doesn't need you.

—I know she needs me, murmured the monk and his face shone calmly.

—How do you know?

—I know. When we're both alone, She and I, She turns a little to the right, like this, and looks at me and smiles, as if She's saying: 'I'm not afraid as long as you're near me.' One day I thought of going to the Monastery. I got up, but just as I stepped over this low stone wall I heard a loud voice behind me:

'Ignatius, where are you going?

'Nowhere, my Mistress,' I said, and came back in.

—And have you been here many years?

—I don't count them. It seems like just a day. I was a young man, twenty years old, when I sat on this step for the first time; now it seems I'm terribly old. But then again, no; my heart is twenty years old.

At this moment I understand how heavy the mystery of confession is. Until now no one knows how I spent my two years at Mount Athos. My friends think I went there to see Byzantine icons, or because of a secret longing to live a bygone era. And now, look, I feel embarrassed to speak.

How shall I put it? I remember a late afternoon in the spring, when a storm overtook me as I was coming down Mount Taygetos, near Pentavli. The whirlwind was so fierce I fell flat on the ground so I wouldn't be blown off the mountain. Lightning encircled me from everywhere and I closed my eyes to keep from being blinded and waited, face down, on the bare earth. The whole towering mountain shook and two fir trees next to me snapped in the middle and crashed to the ground. I felt the thunderbolt's brimstone in the air, and suddenly the deluge broke, the wind died down, and thick warm drops of rain struck the trees and soil. It pelted the thyme, oregano, and sage, and they shook off their odors and scented the whole earth.

I rose to my feet and began to descend the mountain, feeling with acrid delight the huge drops beating on my hair and face and hands. For the first time in my life I felt the touch of the eternal God, the Zeus of Thunder, like a woman. It fell from the heavens like violent love, and Earth and all her creatures steamed under the vigorous thrust from heaven, like Semele.[13] In an hour the sky had cleared, the cuckoo began its song, the towns glistened in the plain below, and at the sea beyond, at the white bubbling seashore, Kardamili[14] could be seen with its Manian towers. And the entire sky in the west turned green and golden.

Yes, this is how those years of monkish solitude seem to me today, like this hour on Mount Taygetos, frightful and sweet, full of love and thunder.

They gave me the cloister of *Prodromos*,[15] the one I had chosen, for my abode. It was just what I wanted—set in a deep thick forest, next to water, amid fruitless trees, firs, elms, beeches, and oaks— closed in like a well with only the sky passing overhead. And at night the stars sparkled.

It had an old cracked chapel and two cells with fireplaces. *Prodromos* next to Christ on the *iconostasis*,[16] looked like a skinny green locust, with two enormous eyes, and as he was poised on the edges of his feet, he seemed not to be walking but leaping from tree to tree. And two massive wings were flapping behind his back like tongues of fire, giving the impression that this small body had caught fire and was burning.

I had arrived at night. The flagstones were damp and wind was funneling through the skylights. I sat down at a crumbling old pew, and a cold shudder gripped my body, a weird terror, and suddenly I could not hold back the tears. I rose from the pew and fell on the stone floor before the *iconostasis* and began to question my soul: Do you believe? Can you give yourself totally? Can you overcome the body?

I wanted this act to be mine, free, like fruit that falls from the vine when ripe. What was I seeking? To become disciplined to an austere rhythm, to enlist in an army that had embarked on the most daring hope. And I, in the Christian Argus, nailing death on the prow, wanted to embark with the fasting, celibate, ragged heroes—straining the red sail to the breaking point, like a heart, and the mystical vine of the Lord's supper would blossom on the mast and we would be corsairs, sailing to seize the golden fleece of immortality from the shoulders of God!

So that I, too, like the ascetics, could overcome pettiness, fear, and death—with faith. United with God, I wanted to feel my every moment, heavy like honey, unwilling to fall, all substance, obedience and passion. Ah, I cried, how can I break the goblets of the mind that contaminate the immortal water, and drink, mouth to mouth, from the source, without questions and doubts, without words and sophistries. With love and faith, simple and straightforward—the way we plunge into the sea, without weighing, struggling, hoping—submitting to the laws.

Ah! Action, the constantly new answer, the daily revelation, the Macedonian sword that undoes the knot.

Jesus, I cried, sprawled out on the stones, gentle countenance of the highest Chimera, Sower, whose hand moved like a vigorous wing and dropped the seed of immortality into that deep little garden, the heart of man that has peace no more—all seeming small to it now, with this Earth no longer able to contain it,

Lord, Lord, like the Bacchante who rises wordless and pale, with bloodstained lips after mercilessly dismembering God while in the act of receiving Him, and with dancing feet and upright breasts turns toward the full moon, her limbs drenched in the cool waters of ecstasy,

similarly, oh, crucified Bacchus, grant that my soul be caught up in your love, and as it hearkens to your voice on high, let it grasp the drums and sweep up the Earth to your rhythm, beyond death!

On the first day I sat quietly and planned my Asceticism. I laid out my program the way I have always liked—with figures, with strict logical tools, with geometrical madness. My plan was simple: "To do whatever I don't like." I would divide myself into two camps: the higher and the lower, the one in the light and the other in the dark, the soul and the body, and I would finally declare open war between them.

I told myself: I shall humble and constrict to the limit the desires of the flesh. Does it want to sleep? I'll stay awake. Does it want to eat? I'll fast. Does it want to sit? I'll get up and climb the mountain. Is it cold? I'll strip and walk on the stones.

I would have to take Asceticism as a method of discipline, the submission of the lower to the higher wheel that grasps the mud as it revolves, and gives it the countenance it wants.

And slowly I would rise to harder labors: When I subdue the flesh I shall turn to the soul and divide it, too, in two camps, lower and higher, human and divine. I shall fight the small spiritual pleasures—reading and recollection, the gratification of victory, justice, friendship and tenderness, joy and sorrow.

And again, if I won for a second time, I would proclaim a new severence within me: Down with hope, the final enemy, while high above me the flame of God would be consuming me, smokeless, without a flicker, in profound darkness and silence.

No! No! I will never divulge the martyrdom and ecstasy in the deep pit of this cloister. Not because I don't want to or don't dare, but because the martyrdom is unspeakable and there are no human words capable of containing its delight.

After three months I could no longer stand on my feet from the fasting and hardships. My eyes had grown wild from lack of sleep, my ears were buzzing, my arms and legs had become like a grasshopper's. But there were times at night, after the sun had set, when I felt two enormous flames on my back like wings.

And my soul beat hard within me and in her lonliness cried out before the threshold:

From this deep cellar where they've buried me, like the kindled torch that refuses to be rubbed in the ground and snuffed out,

I leap straight up and grasp the narrow skylight, and with my brains purified by divine vigil, prop myself up and perceive the whole earth from afar!

Neither solitude with her harsh, friendly hand on my shoulder as we wander the uncut forest together, nor the triple-layered silence that nourishes my mind, nor hope that has finally ripened and angrily bites the breast's nipple, now firmly seeking food to sate her hunger,

can drown the invincible cry inside me.

I worked my body on anxiety and hope, my chest

collapsed and my feet spread and hardened from treading the stones, and I became like the sword that cuts the night in two.

They assigned me the task of grinding, night and day, and their laughter and games reach down to this jail of mine.

But I hang my head between my bony knees, growling like a tethered bitch, and I grind their loss. I am a princess and do not fall low. Steady! Eyes open, the heart a steel slate, writes. What do you see?

I see the shame, I see the cities, I see life pitching her motley tent at every junction. You don't select. You fornicate with eagle and snail alike. You've become a crossroad and the four winds pounce on you and you've filled the earth with she- and he-bastards!

It's time for the uproarious feast to break up, oh, Babylon, and for the lash to whistle in the air, and for that enormous spark, my spirit, to pounce on your buttresses and rush through your streets, burning your wooden gods and melting the golden calves and tangling your reins

while you grow hoarse begging for mercy.

But the spirit doesn't stop, it ignites because the breath of God fans it furiously from behind, like a whirlwind.

Ah! Ah! I can feel your hot ashes fitting right into this small palm of my hand!

I flung my cries out boldly so as not to hear the high relentless voice inside me—like a man who sings in the dark to hide his fear. Temptation prowled around my cloister like a hungry lion. How many times I felt him, with terror, enter my cell and enrich my sleep, and at midnight in the moonlight, fill the slope with women and with laughter and wooden clogs!

He'd come like St. Basil, joyful, open-armed, laying all the joys of the world on my pillow; he'd come with songs, with laughter, or quietly, gentle-spoken, he'd touch my flesh with a downy softness, like a female breast. Ah! One night I remember I was on the floor listening for him because he was late in coming.

And the quiet voice rose inside me then and spoke:

—Hypocrite, you leave the door open behind you and furtively close one eye and say: I'll leave when I'm tired playing games. Close the door, by god!

—What door? I murmured, trembling.

—What door? I'll tell you , my brave braggart! An ascetic in Thebes grafted leprosy on himself. He took out the sickle knife that he used for pruning trees and castrated himself—now, there's someone who closed the door behind him. Do you hear? Can you do this? You tremble. Is it barbaric? Then be silent! Become whatever you wish—monk or prior or patriarch—go to it!

A few days later a heavy nightmare settled over me, as I was leaning against the pew. I was still awake, my eyes were open, and I could see and hear: I saw myself entering my paternal home. My father was sitting cross-legged, as was his custom, on the corner of the couch. When he caught sight of me he jumped up savagely and began to shout:

—You've bothered to come—and wearing a cassock, too? You're disgusted with the world? Where did you learn about the world? Did you marry or ever lose a child? Did you enjoy life? Did you work? Go away so I won't have to see you!

Then the old man sat down and broke into hideous laughter.

—Where do you invite me? he resumed, more softly. Where do you invite me? To your wedding? I'll hire violins, I'll slaughter lambs, I'll summon dancers! And I'll remember my own youth. My son, my only son is getting married. He'll have children, I'll overcome death.

He turned slowly and looked at me, then lapsed into a long silence. A tear fell from his eyes. Sweetness and tenderness overcame him and he began to speak in a grieved tone:

—How did you come to me like this, my son, weak-blooded, without strength? Your hair has already begun to thin out, your eyes have dimmed, you're growing stooped, you've wrapped yourself in a cassock and rattle on doors like a beggar. So my lineage has dried up, eh? What did you do with the blood I gave you?

And quietly, like hoarfrost, it all dissolved in the air; the vision vanished and the voice disappeared.

I know, Kosmas will say that all these visions and voices were creations of fantasy, hallucinations of a body that was hungry, thirsty, sleepless, and longing for sin.

But in those hours I was living so profoundly that I didn't give name to joys and sorrows, and in naming them gain comfort; but I lived them unbaptized, ungoverned, all flux, feeling, and vertigo. As though I lived everything musically, deeper than the word, with diaphanous body, all motion and rhythm. I was plunged in an ocean of sound and light; but, even the light became rhythm and beat on my temples.

Now that I reflect on it, words seem like exorcisms to me. As soon as you pronounce them, demons— good and evil—squeeze inside these exorcisms, bind and imprison themselves, and lose their power. This is the mission of words, and of bodies, too.

But as soon as the spirit, taking courage, breaks the jails and joins the formidable forces that leap out, how miserable all formalities and sophistries appear,

Kosmas, like nothing more than insipid paper consolations. It's as if you'd been hungry all your life and in order to belie your hunger were fed the menu and you, like a goat, chewed it like cud. But now, behold, for the first time, by throwing away the paper naming the foods, you taste the true meat and wheat bread and you drink the true water—and everything at once becomes blood inside you, and love and invisible powers.

I got up trembling, feeling my father's shadow heavy upon me. I don't ever remember him saying a tender word, or caressing me; I remember him harsh and unsmiling, handing down the flame of the race to me, commanding me to outdo them all in strength and pride and stubbornness. One day as he watched me, stooped and sallow from reading, he said to me angrily: "Go out and play, laugh, climb a mountain and limber up your blood, make love, fight with your friends, breathe some clean air. I'm going to burn all that paper rubbish of yours. God bless the hand of your grandfather who broke down the doors of the Osios Lucas Monastery in the Great Uprising of '21[17] and tied up the monks who resisted, and tore their ancient books and ascetic biographies and passed them around to his brave men who rammed them all against the clove trees with the butts of their guns and used them to shoot at the Turks." This is how those men upheld tradition, in an even loftier way, by killing the barbarians with their books.

Ah! how the voice of my father, like the greatest tempter, greater even than woman, broke thus suddenly into my solitude:

Get up! You're seeking God? Here He is! He's action, full of mistakes, gropings, perseverance and struggle. God is not the force that found eternal harmony, but the force that eternally breaks every harmony, always seeking something higher. And the person who struggles and moves forward in his narrow circle with this method finds God and works with him.

Get up, go mingle with people, learn to love them and kill them—love is reverence, affection and disgust. Don't expect to give birth to anything by yourself. You will raise yourself only by struggling with men, pitying and despising our miserable heart. Come, whole, with all your weaknesses, misgivings and illusions. You will be purified by struggling. What are you waiting for? The enemy walks our streets, tramples our homes and our hearts. Come, you, too, choose your bulwark and shoot. The enemy is God with the cassocks and knotted cord, the unwashed, unwed and lazy!

And I thought:

If only one morning I could suddenly enter the Macedonian village where Kosmas, transformed into a teacher, is working, preparing a revolution. And I could open the door and he should see me abruptly before him. Ah! The two men who harness themselves to the plough like God's good team. And to sit down again with geometric madness, just as God does, to prepare the plan and to divide the danger!

And to stand over the paper you're bending over and struggling with, Petros, and tell you:

—Put away Art, that gleaming Siren; the time has not yet come for song. Come, walk with me on earth and work, and when, indeed, your heart overflows, find relief in discharging a courageous act.

The days and months passed. Sickness came. Delirium. I recall an old hermit, *Yero*-Manasis,[18] who came and kept vigil over me. And as I began to get well, he left and I never saw him again. My body resisted desperately, and was able to save itself. I rose from the planks where I was lying and began to walk.

Spring came; the air grew warm, the swallows returned, the caterpillars abandoned their humble nature in the earth, clad themselves in the brilliant clothing of marriage and death, and began to play in the sun. The earth covered itself with daisies and chamomile, countless insects merged under the new leaves without stirring. Far away, in the protection of a Monastery courtyard some lemon trees had blossomed, and when the wind blew, their fragrance passed over me like a wave.

I had taken a long walk that day; like the earth's insect I, too, rejoiced in the warmth of the sun and was coming to life. A poplar tree had bloomed and was filled with frizzly leaves like the open wings of a butterfly. I felt my strength spilling into the soil and rising more clearly in that direction. I grew tired. I wanted to lie down and close my eyes. "It's spring," I reasoned. "It's spring, the Great Tempter. The monks cannot hinder it from walking on their solitude. Even the most decrepit body goes out on its doorstep and warms itself. And even the toughest skin on the human body suddenly blooms and, trembling, the hermit beholds the red fruit."

There was a monk who, for fifty years had eaten no bread nor drunk wine; he fed himself on chaff and salt water. His eyebrows covered his eyes and his whiskers ran like a river on the earth. The angels feared him and came down to receive his commands.

One spring afternoon, watching the birds building and warbling, and the worms coming together, he said with pride: "I subdued spring."

He rose and began walking along the seashore and as he looked down he found a woman's silk slipper in the sand; the entire seashore glowed and filled with shouts of laughter. He returned to his cell in agitation, to fall at his icon stand and exorcise the evil, but just outside his doorstep, seated near the well, he saw a veiled woman, weeping.

"Show love, old man, servant of God," she said, "and receive me in your cell; I lost my way, it's dark and if I remain outside the beasts will eat me. Don't feel disgust for your servant; I, too, am a creature of God."

She was wearing a djellaba, like a fellaha, and as she finished talking a wind came up and lifted her djellaba—and she was wearing nothing else. The hermit wasn't quick enough to close his eyes not to see, and he saw, and he fell into sin and said: "How good woman's body is!" And at once the woman disappeared from before him—because she was the Tempter—and the monk fell to the ground in convulsions begging for forgiveness. But his God was angry and gave orders and Satan took his soul at that same instant.

I felt dizzy and leaned against a tree. I was watching the birds gathering dirt and hairs and little branches, and building rapidly. All the soil was stirring, full of living things and working, and I could feel the tree upon which I leaned raising sap to its peak, struggling to transubstantiate the mud, stone, water, air and sun and make them into blossoms. I was watching matter, the great harlot, with the broad haunches, falling at the feet of Christ, like Mary Magdalene, weepingly being transubstantiated.

Deep compassion overtook me for Earth who carries us all, and nourishes us.

Unutterable sadness weighed on my heart because I often spoke ill of you, oh, Earth, oh, Mother, I who throb in your bowels, full of soil and dewiness!

The good horseman on his unbridled rampaging horse, holds a brimming cup of water and doesn't allow even a drop to spill—likewise, oh, Mistress Amazon, in your surging ascent, hold the heart of man steady, firm, full!

Calm the heart of the rabbit under the fern, keep sickness far from the pine, firmly establish the sperm in the male and implant veins of milk in the breasts of woman.

A single song from the earthy heart of life defeats the most deadly sin; Lord! Lord! give heed to the song that Earth warbles, caught in the snare of death. And weakened as I was from hunger, and enchanted by Spring, I understood at that moment the oft-sung melody of Earth, coming from thousands of lips, from small creatures and beasts, from the waters and plants and men, as it bounced resoundingly, brisk, far off and inside me, like an invocation, a command and reproach.

Ah! the sweetness of life! How carefree Earth

sings—like the scarlet-throated goldfinch that sits and warbles, carried away by the scent of springtime's wild pear tree and by the warm nest swaying overhead, with the two shiny eggs in the middle. It raises its crimson throat and says: "I'll sing, and then I'll warm them; but I'll sing first!"

and it hasn't understood that it is sitting on the hunter's snare!

NOTES

1. Emmanuel H. Kasdaglis also assisted in the publishing of Nikos Kazantzakis' complete works.

2. Nikos Saklampanis, now an attorney living in Crete, is the nephew of Nikos Kazantzakis, and the grandson of Mihali Kazantzakis.

3. For example, the lines "Ah, what is this good, that I cannot rise from sheer sweetness of the air . . ." are the opening words of Magdalene in her first monologue in the tragedy *Christos* (*Theatro*, a collection of tragedies, Athens, 1956, page 16).

4. Mrs. Helen Kazantzakis suggests that Kazantzakis may not have forgotten the *Symposium* but may have thought the manuscript lost and "did not like to think over a thing that had no remedy." Or, she adds, he may have forgotten it as he did other lost works, including a tragedy-comedy, a Sartrian one-act *Huis Clos*, written some forty years before Sartre and Beckett.

5. *Nikos Kazantzakis—A Biography*, by Helen Kazantzakis (Simon & Schuster, New York, 1968).

6. Pandelis Prevelakis is a prominent writer in Greece today. He worked on several projects with Nikos Kazantzakis.

7. Letter from Nikos Kazantzakis to the Reverend Emmanuel Papastefanou, Berlin, September 5, 1922:

"Brother Papastefanou: Seldom has a letter touched me as your last letter did. I was plunged in loneliness and shouting the Word to the stones and waters. I was saying: Our first duty is to shout, to shout in our loneliness! My God, how lonely I was, certain and despairing! Here, Frankdom is rotting. All the works of art that even last year deeply moved me and filled my heart, have no significance for me this year. They seem narrow to me and no longer worthy of the contemporary marvelous hope of man. The paintings are beautiful, and so is the music and the songs, and Dante and Homer . . . but all of this now appears to me like an empty serpent's skin, like stereotyped forms of a body that has passed, and restless, naked, shivering in the hostile air, struggles now to create the new birth.

. . . I roam the streets like Mahomet, who ran about breaking all the false gods of Kaaba with his iron cane. After seven years of preaching he had only eleven followers, and most of them were women. Oh! The day they chased them out and the eleven homes were closed and they took the road of exile! Oh, God, when will the persecution begin for us, too? But first the preaching has to start. I feel I'm going to die from agony. I feel weak, I don't have the strength to begin. My mind is armed to the teeth, but I just can't make that formidable leap.* I battle here, I

*See *Letters to Galatea*, Athens, 1958, p. 150.

lay siege to the crucial moment. I fell ill. Now I've grown stronger again and continue the battle. I tell myself: I shall finish the *Symposium*, a book I am writing, comments on our religion, on our Creed and our Decalogue. We (you, Leftheris, Sfakianakis, Sikelianos and two women) speak of God at a dinner. Just as Plato spoke of love, we speak of God. This is why I fervently beseech you to write me about your theogony in as great detail as you can, thus you will greatly help me put the words in your mouth that match you exactly. Each of us is going to incarnate the new countenance of the Fighter in accordance with his particular spirit.

On a piece of paper, I am writing you my tentative formulation of my decalogue. It would be well for each of us to create a 'Creed,' a 'Decalogue,' a dogma, to think out all of our religion—and then at a Synod, which we will have, to make the definitive formulation. To make it easier, I have separated the material as follows:

1. Essence of divinity (struggle, pain, joy, hope, etc.)

2. Relationship between God and man: religion, art, metaphysics.

3. Relationship between man and man. Ethics, philosophy, love (erotas).

4. Relationship between man and nature: experience, science, identity. All is one.

We shall organize the Greeks in leagues, 'All Those Living,' in ranks.*

The first, self-evident—for the education of the people, intellectual, economic, political, and religious freedom.

The second, mystical: revolution, the overthrow of contemporary life.

*Ion Dragoumis wrote a book in 1911 with the title, *All Those Living*.

The third, more mystical yet, ours: Religion."
(Attached to the letter was the following Decalogue, with a notation made by Helen Kazantzakis at the top: "The Decalogue that Nikos Kazantzakis referred to in his letter.")

I   I am the Combatant. I suffer ceaselessly. I rejoice and hope. I am not omnipotent. Inwardly enslaved, I battle for liberation.

II   You are my Father and my Son, the Co-worker, Lover, Bridegroom. Struggle with me.

III From You is suspended the salvation of Heaven and Earth. In every moment, you carry the whole world on your shoulders.

IV   Listen to your heart and follow me. Sacrifice is my way. Crush your body and regain your vision. We are all one.

V   Love man because you are he.

VI   Love the animals and the plants because you were they, and now they follow you as faithful co-workers and slaves.

VII Love your body. Only with it, will you be able to battle and give spirit to matter on this Earth.

VIII Love matter. Within it, I hide and battle. Liberate me.

IX   Guard valiantly the straits that I entrusted to you in battle. We could be saved, we could be lost. It depends on us.

X   Await death with confidence. It is the Nobleman of choice. It is I, enlisting the Order of the immortals.

(For the reader who is interested in making the comparison, the above Decalogue appears in revised form in various stages throughout the *Saviors of God*.)

8. The two letters by Emmanuel Papastefanou show a highly romantic inclination. Accompanying the two letters, Mrs. Kazantzakis attached a portion of a letter Nikos Kazantzakis wrote to Emmanuel Papastefanou, cautioning him against this overromanticizing. See Note 9.

9. Portion of letter from Nikos Kazantzakis to the Rev. Papastefanou: ". . . I write to you again hurriedly about our struggle. Be careful. When you are trying to capture the countenance of our God, avoid whatever you have learned about the Christian God. Our God is not all-good, he is not all-mighty, he is not all-beautiful, he is not all-wise. If he were, of what value would our collaboration with him be? If he were, how could he feel pain, how could he struggle, how could he keep rising? Avoid romantic theologies, human hopes, the certainties that are always held by the cowardly—either optimists or pessimists. Nothing is certain in the universe, we throw ourselves into the uncertainty, gambling our fate every second; we exert pressure on the Universe to lose or save itself. We have an enormous responsibility. Because there is no certainty either for destruction or salvation. We collaborate with the one current—and whichever wins!"

10. The name Arpagos was probably arrived at from the words ἁρπαγἡ or ἅρπαξ, which literally mean rapaciousness, or one who plunders or seizes by force. Kazantzakis often referred to himself as a rapacious soul, with a voracious and insatiable appetite to grasp and experience and know everything he could. In a chapter on Cavafy in his book, *Journeying* (Little, Brown and Company, Boston, 1975), he describes this rapacious feeling at a farewell dinner attended by the young intellectuals of Alexandria . . . how he is anxious and rapacious in their presence, and how he

delights in literally grasping by force the intense, rigid, uncompromising ideas of the young.

11. Ion Dragoumis (1878–1920), descendant of a prominent Macedonian family, served as Consul General in Vienna and Berlin, and also in the embassies of Constantinople, Rome, and London. Exiled to Corsica in 1917, he returned to Athens that same year. He worked toward unifying the people of Anatolia, and forming an Anatolian Confederation. He died in Athens, the victim of a political assassination.

12. Angelos Sikelianos (1884–1951), was one of the major poets of modern Greece. So high was Kazantzakis' esteem for Sikelianos that when the Society of Letters was ready to propose Kazantzakis as the candidate for the Nobel Prize, he made the stipulation that he would accept the prize only if it were shared with Sikelianos.

13. Idas, son of Aphareus and cousin of Castor and Pollux in Greek mythology. Killed by Zeus.

14. Pandelis Prevelakis notes that Arpagos lauds Kosmas with words that recall the article Kazantzakis dedicated to Ion Dragoumis on the occasion of the sixth year after his death (published in the *Free Press*, Athens, August 1, 1926). See Kazantzakis, "Esoteric Biographical Sketch" by Prevelakis, preface to *Four Hundred Letters of Kazantzakis to Prevelakis* (Athens, 1965).

15. *Six Poets of Modern Greece*, translated and introduced by Edmund Keeley and Philip Sherrard (Alfred A. Knopf, New York, 1961).

CHAPTER 1

1. Lord . . . Lord . . .
2. Lithari—a game in which the players compete in a stone-throwing contest; a modern version of the ancient discus-throwing contests.

CHAPTER 2

1. Misiriou—referring to the Nile River.
2. Romaic—refers to the Contemporary Greek; also the Greek during the Turkish occupation.
3. Rumeli is the central part of Greece. Its name is derived from the Turkish, *Rum ili*, which means country of the Greeks. During the Turkish occupation, the mountains of Rumeli were the center of guerilla activity preceding the war for independence. Diakos, Androutsos, Panagourias, Gouros, Thiovouniotis, Karaiskakis, and other Greek heroes of the revolution fought there.
4. Aivali (Kythoniais) is a city in Asia Minor across from Mytelene. In 1914 and 1922 it was the site of the slaughter of Greeks by the Turks.
5. Proussa (Bythinia in ancient times) is a city in Asia Minor south of the Bosporus and Sea of Marmora. It was a major battle site against the Turks in 1922.
6. Kastoria is a city on the Greek Albanian-Serbian border, and the site of activities during the Turkish occupation. It was the center of guerrilla warfare and all nationalistic resistance against the Turks and Bulgarians.
7. Joachim III (1834–1912), was the ecumenical patriarch of Constantinople from 1878 to 1884. Forced to resign in

1884, he lived in Constantinople for five years and then went to Mt. Athos in 1889 where he lived a total of thirteen years in exile. He was recalled as Patriarch and reigned as one of the great spiritual leaders until his death in 1912.

8. Kampayia—red shoes worn by Byzantine emperors.

9. Polis—refers to Constantinople, the most important city in Byzantine history. It was the capital of the Byzantine Empire (330–1453) and later of the Ottoman Empire (1453–1923). Today it is Istanbul, belonging to Turkey.

10. Aghia Sophia—Church of the Holy Wisdom in Constantinople. Once the throne of the ecumenical patriarch of the Greek Orthodox Church, today it is a Turkish mosque. However, the city of Constantinople (Istanbul) is still one of the five Eastern Orthodox Patriarchal Sees.

11. Psalm 24, 7.
"Lift up your heads, O gates!
and be lifted up, O ancient doors!
that the King of glory may come in."

12. From the Collect added to the Salutations to the Virgin Mary (Akathist Hymn) in A.D. 626 in recognition of a miracle attributed to the Mother of God.

The Akathist Hymn (Akathistos Hymnos) is a profound devotional poem which sings the praises of the Holy Mother. It is a composite work probably of the fifth or sixth century, composed of twenty-four stanzas. It is divided into four parts, each of which is recited on one of the first four Fridays during the Lenten season in the Greek Orthodox Church. The entire hymn is sung on the fifth Friday of Lent.

About the year A.D. 626, the year the Avars and the Persians attacked Constantinople, Sergius, the then Patriarch, led the frightened populace in a great procession

around the walls of the city as they sang and carried icons
of the Lord and the Virgin. Strengthened by their religious
faith and aided by a tempest which destroyed many enemy
ships, the people of Constantinople put the barbarians to
flight. They considered their deliverance a miracle and in
thanksgiving gathered in the Church of Aghia Sophia, and
standing with reverence throughout the night, sang hymns
of thanksgiving and praise to the Virgin Mary. Hence the
title of the Hymn, Akathistos, from the Greek word for
"not seated."

Collect: "To thee the Champion Leader, do I thy City
ascribe thank offerings and victory, for thou, oh,
Mother of God has delivered me from sufferings,
but as thou hast Invincible power, do thou free me
from every kind of danger, so that to thee, I may
cry Hail, thou Bride unwed."

13. Akrita—a frontier guard during the Byzantine era. It
has since become the name of many Greek heroes.

14. Apelatiki—a nail-studded, macelike weapon used by
the Byzantine frontier guards.

15. Genos—race (birth, origin)

16. Romiosini—the contemporary Greek race, with
strong overtones of Greekdom under Turkish domination.
A bittersweet word evoking deep emotions in the modern
Greek. Implicit in its meaning is a memory of struggle,
humiliation, pride, and hope in the perpetuation of the
Greek spirit—a shared brotherhood under foreign subjuga-
tion.

17. Greek Independence Day from Turkish rule.

18. The beginning verse of the Greek national anthem.
The patriotic poem, "Hymn to Victory," written by the
poet Dionysios Solomos in 1823, officially became the

Greek national anthem by royal command on June 28, 1865.

19. Mountains north and northeast of Salonika, which were sites of resistance activity against the Turks from the sixteenth century on, and again against the German invasion in 1941.

20. Strimonas and Vardaris are large rivers flowing into the Aegean, one to the east and one to the west of Salonika.

21. Efthini—obligation, duty, responsibility.

22. Xeniou Dia refers to the Zeus of hospitality.

23. Mani is in southern Peloponnesos, ending at the edge of Tainaron. During the Ottoman occupation, it was essentially only a tributary. An area on which no Turk set foot during the Turkish occupation of Greece.

24. Episcopacy—surveillance from a superior position.

25. Frankia is a name Greeks use for Western Europe. It refers to the Franks who decimated the country in the thirteenth century.

26. See Chapter 2, Note 16.

CHAPTER 3

1. Mistra, adjacent to Sparta, at the northern edge of Mani, became the new center of the Byzantine world after the fall of Constantinople. Today tourists flock to this picturesque site to view the ruins of the fourteenth century renaissance of Greek culture.

2. This phrase refers to the isolation of man from the world, and his union with the one. It dates back to

Plotinus, A.D. 205–270 (see *Enneads*, Latin 5, paragraph 11, Brehier in Paris, 1938, page 188). Also in the writings of St. Gregory of Nyssa who refers to the flight of Moses toward the alone. In Indian philosophy it refers to the ideal union of man in his flight of the one to the one.

3. Askisi—ascetic discipline, exercise.

4. Nike—the goddess of victory.

5. Panaghia Portaitisa—the Virgin of the Gate, an icon at the Monastery of Iviron on the Holy Mountain. Legend has it that it miraculously escaped destruction during the reign of Theophilos the Iconoclast in the ninth century, and found its way across the sea to the Iviron Monastery, where it stands guard over the gate of the monastery to this day.

6. Glykofilusa—the Virgin of the Tender Kiss. Another icon, according to legend, that escaped destruction during the reign of Theophilos the Iconoclast, and mysteriously found its way to the Holy Mountain where it remains to this day. It shows the Virgin wearing a crown, and the Christ child reaching up with His left hand, stroking His mother's chin.

7. Damala—a Greek word for cow. In many biblical references, Christ is referred to as a calf. The word Damala evokes an image of the Virgin mourning her slaughtered calf.

8. Korfiatissa—the Virgin of the Mountaintops.

9. Panaghia is the name given to the Virgin Mary. It literally means all-holy.

10. Yerakokoudouna—bronze bells on Cretan lyres.

11. Tsaprassia—knee-plates of silver or some other metal, tied in place with strings, worn by soldiers in Byzantine times, partly for ornament and partly to protect their knees in battle.

12. Lavras—a monastic colony.

13. Semele was the mistress of Zeus by whom she gave birth to Dionysos. Before the child's birth, she implored Zeus to reveal himself to her in all his magnificence and she died, consumed by the divine fire she herself provoked.

14. Kardamili is a city on the coast of Peloponnesos, southeast of Sparta.

15. Prodromos—John the Baptist, the Forerunner.

16. Iconostasis—the partition in the Greek Orthodox Church that separates the sanctuary from the nave of the church. The major icons of the church are positioned here. The iconostasis has an opening at the center (Holy Gate) and to its right is always positioned the icon of Jesus Christ, and to His right, the icon of John the Baptist. To the left of the Gate is the icon of the Virgin Mary, and to her left, usually an icon of the patron saint of the church. On the two doors to the left and right of the iconostasis appear the icons of Archangels Michael and Gabriel.

17. The rebellion of the Greeks against their Turkish oppressors in 1821, leading to their eventual liberation.

18. Yero—the Greek word meaning *old.*

ABOUT THE AUTHOR

THE LATE NIKOS KAZANTZAKIS is best known in the United States as the author of *Zorba the Greek*, *The Greek Passion* (filmed under the title "He Who Must Die"), and *Freedom or Death*.

Born in Crete in 1883, he spent most of his adult life in travel. He studied at the University of Athens where he received his law degree, and in Paris, with the philosopher Henri Bergson. Later he went to Germany and Italy where he pursued studies in literature and art. He lived and traveled in Spain, England, Russia, Egypt, Israel, China, and Japan. For a short while in 1945, he served as Greek Minister of Education, and was president of the Greek Society of Men of Letters. In 1947–1948 he was Director of UNESCO's Department of Translations of the Classics.

Among the numerous novels, dramas, books of travel and poetry that comprise his writings, one of his greatest achievements is the monumental epic *The Odyssey: A Modern Sequel*, a work which was twelve years in the making. Numbered among his many translations into modern Greek verse are works of Homer, Plato, Dante, Faust, Nietzsche, Darwin, Bergson, and others.

Acclaimed as one of the most eminent and versatile writers of our time, he has earned the highest praise from critics and scholars in Europe and America, and from such of his peers as Albert Schweitzer, Thomas Mann, and Albert Camus, to whom he narrowly lost the Nobel Prize in 1951.

He died in Germany in 1957.